A Trilogy to Define, Plan, and Contact Center

1) 42 Rules for Using AI in Your Contact Center

Artificial Intelligence (AI) is a transformative force in contact centers, revolutionizing customer interactions. AI tools, including chatbots, virtual assistants, and data analysis capabilities, automate processes, streamline interactions, and offer real-time language translation. These technologies enhance customer experiences by providing personalized services and anticipating needs. The evolving integration of AI holds the potential to create a customer-centric environment, surpassing traditional practices. "42 Rules for Using AI in Your Contact Center" delves into AI's potential impact on customers in The Fourth Industrial Era.

2) 42 Rules for Planning AI in Your Contact Center

Planning for AI in your contact center demands a comprehensive strategy. It goes beyond merely automating agent tasks and requires a focused roadmap to address specific challenges and deliver ROI. Your plan should outline goals, align business and tech objectives, assess your environment, define performance metrics, evaluate AI tech, organize data, and set implementation timelines. "42 Rules for Planning AI in Your Contact Center" provides a roadmap to reduce uncertainties and solve specific problems to yield significant business advantages.

3) 42 Rules to Manage an AI Center of Excellence for Your Contact Center

AI Centers of Excellence (CoE) manage emerging technologies, skills, or disciplines that defy traditional organizational structures. They provide governance, prioritize efforts, and steer businesses away from focusing solely on technology over practical applications. Establishing an AI-CoE for contact centers demands a focused strategy tailored to customer engagement dynamics. It requires meticulous planning, a clear vision, and alignment with broader business goals. Serving as a hub for AI strategy, an AI-CoE ensures initiatives align with business objectives, offers expertise, and guides departments through the complex AI landscape. "42 Rules to Manage an AI Center of Excellence for Your Contact Center" delves into key pillars such as strategic alignment, technology, governance, data, analytics, talent, security, and privacy.

42 Rules for Planning AI in Your Contact Center
(Book 2 of 3)

An overview of how to plan for artificial intelligence and prepare your data in your contact center

By Geoffrey A. Best

E-mail: info@superstarpress.com
20660 Stevens Creek Blvd., Suite 210
Cupertino, CA 95014

Published by SuperStar Press™, a THiNKaha® imprint
20660 Stevens Creek Blvd., Suite 210, Cupertino, CA 95014
https://42rules.com

First Printing: March 2024
Paperback ISBN: 978-1-60773-128-3   1-60773-128-2
eBook ISBN: 978-1-60773-127-6   1-60773-127-4
Place of Publication: Silicon Valley, California, USA
Library of Congress Number: 2023924065

Trademarks

Warning and Disclaimer

Praises for This Book

"Geoffrey Best isn't just an expert; he's a pioneer in the realm of AI-driven contact center transformation. As an early adopter, he's been at the forefront, blending real-world experience with groundbreaking innovation. In *42 Rules for Planning AI in Your Contact Center*, he shares a unique blend of hands-on insights and visionary foresight. While Geoffrey's recommendations are rooted in practicality, he never shies away from pushing the technological envelope, charting a path for the rest of us. If you want a deep dive into how AI can revolutionize customer service, guided by someone who's been in the trenches yet always looks to the horizon, Geoffrey's book is indispensable. He truly is a beacon in the ever-evolving world of AI."
Robert Bolen, Sales-First Technology CEO, Founder/CEO, Bunch Inc., MS Innovation and Entrepreneurship, HEC Paris

"Geoffrey has written a concise and insightful book that provides a practical and thorough roadmap for organizations looking to integrate artificial intelligence into their contact centers. Beginning from defining business objectives through the need for continual innovation post-deployment, this book lays out a methodical, step-by-step, structured blueprint for the implementation of AI in a contact center environment. The author has a remarkable ability to break down complex technical concepts into simple, easy-to-understand ideas, making them accessible to a wide audience without requiring prior expertise in IT or technology. Most importantly, each of the 42 rules presented in this book is not just informative but also actionable. In conclusion, Geoffrey provides a strong foundation for those beginning their journey into the world of artificial intelligence. He is a must-read for anyone interested in leveraging AI to enhance customer service."
John Julia, Vice President of Sales, Thinc Forward

"With the explosion of AI, business leaders need a well-structured plan to guide them. *42 Rules for Planning AI in Your Contact Center* takes you through a comprehensive journey. Geoffrey doesn't just stop at the theoretical level. He dives into the factors that leaders need to consider, offering a comprehensive plan that removes the noise and focuses on what truly matters. This roadmap arms you with where to begin, factors to consider, and how it builds a more personalized experience when done right! The result is a guide that is informative and incredibly practical, making it an indispensable tool. This is a must-read for business, technology, and CX leaders navigating this paradigm shift."
John Maylath, Co-Founder and Managing Partner, AdvisoryHub

"Failure of management to plan for the future and to foresee problems has brought about waste of manpower, of materials, and of machine-time, all of which raise the manufacturer's cost and price that the purchaser must pay. The consumer is not always willing to subsidize this waste. The inevitable result is loss of market. Loss of market begets unemployment."
W. Edwards Deming

Dedication

To Nurcan, my wife, proofreader, and critic. To a technology that continues to evolve without end and challenge all of us. And to my colleagues, family, and friends, who continue to encourage me to document the journey.

Contents

Introduction

Integrating Artificial Intelligence (AI) into a contact center requires a thorough and strategic plan. Contact centers are undergoing a paradigm shift toward cloud-based solutions, facilitating the ease of integrating AI. At the same time, your customers now expect instant answers to their questions without waiting on hold, regardless of the time of day.

Planning for this paradigm shift will involve assessing your contact center's specific needs, understanding the capabilities of AI solutions, and creating a smooth transition process. By doing so, your business can empower your agents, streamline workflows, and provide exceptional customer service.

In my book, *42 Rules for Using AI in Your Contact Center*, I described the possibilities of using AI in contact centers. Here, I present how to plan for an AI-powered contact center that can revolutionize customer interactions, enhancing efficiency, personalizing experiences, and improving overall satisfaction.

Planning for an AI-powered contact center requires exploring critical topics for a well-structured roadmap, which should be more than replacing contact center agents with automation. Your roadmap needs to concentrate on solving specific problems that yield a positive return on investment (ROI) or provide a significant business advantage. Plan to document — your goals, coordinate your business and technology objectives, assess your environment, identify your performance indicators, evaluate AI technologies, organize your data, and establish a timetable for implementation.

The economics of cloud computing for implementing AI and machine learning (ML) are favorable. The availability of scalable computing and massive storage capacity in cloud environments has made AI feasible and economically sensible. Large-scale computing resources with immense machine processing abilities can accomplish even the most complex tasks in seconds. This represents a significant evolution in computing power, making it an opportune time to plan how AI can optimize business processes and improve customer experience.

Major cloud providers offer a range of comprehensive AI and ML services for Automatic Speech Recognition (ASR), Natural Language Processing (NLP) with sentiment analysis, Natural Language Generation (NLG), and tools to build, train, and deploy custom machine-learning models. Moreover, AI/ML providers continue to add new offerings to their services. Thus, as part of your planning, evaluating the capabilities of the cloud providers is a must to understand the range of AI services available for your business.

Finally, understand that data is the foundation of AI. Only recently, creating a data model was a daunting and expensive task. Now, according to Gartner, technological advancements have made big data solutions more accessible, creating the new role known as "citizen data scientist," which Gartner defines as *someone who creates or generates models that leverage predictive or prescriptive analytics, but whose primary job function is outside the field of statistics and analytics.*" As a result, power users can now perform the work of data scientists.

AI is no longer a nice-to-have for contact centers. It has become a necessity. For most companies, just getting started is the most challenging part. However, by beginning the journey, you initiate a process that generates significant short-term improvements and substantial longer-term benefits.

Start Your Plan

Planning is all about a vision to create goals and targets and then map out a way to reach them. Planning never ends. It is continual. You may have a project deliverable but fail to deliver your goal.

Initiating your plan for an AI-powered contact center requires an outline of what you want to achieve, the scope of your current functionality, and your desired outcomes. While your AI implementation may align with a migration to a cloud-based vendor, planning AI still requires a well-defined plan following a sequence of actions with a clear and specific purpose. Your project needs to include selecting appropriate technology, data model development, integration with existing infrastructure and software, testing, agent training, continuous monitoring, and procedures for constant improvement. A well-structured plan facilitates project execution by providing a roadmap to reduce uncertainties. A plan minimizes the chances of rework, confusion, and delays, leading to improved efficiency and productivity during the project. During this planning, consider limiting your scope to avoid "scope creep," a phenomenon that refers to the project expanding beyond its initial boundaries. A well-defined plan will help maintain focus and prevent unnecessary changes that may lead to delays and increased costs.

Planning for AI starts with a comprehensive assessment of your contact center's infrastructure and operational processes. This is essential and helps identify pain points, areas for improvement, and specific AI implementation goals. Next, plan to select the right AI technologies. This includes choosing a suitable AI platform or framework that aligns with the contact center's needs. Consider a proof-of-concept (PoC) to ensure factors like compatibility with current systems and proficiency in handling substantial amounts of data. Your PoC should provide insight into the total cost of ownership with an estimated budget to avoid overspending and effective financial control. A PoC should include defining the tasks for constructing and preparing AI models for voice recognition, natural language processing, sentiment analysis, and customer intent prediction tasks. As the next step, plan to integrate your PoC with your existing contact center infrastructure. Integration involves connecting the AI models with the contact center's communication channels, such as phone systems, chat platforms, and email systems. Involve your business and work with your Information Technology (IT) team to ensure there is communication between everyone involved.

Plan to emphasize data preparation, which may consume a large amount of your time. AI relies heavily on data, and you should expect your datasets to be flawed. Plan procedures for data collection, cleansing, formatting, categorizing, and maintaining. Prepare to continuously monitor for data drift to ensure your data model remains relevant and to track metrics and quality. Any degradation in data quality can lead to inferior model performance, flawed insights, and erroneous decision-making.

Scaling your PoC to a full implementation comes with its own associated challenges. Plan for rigorous testing and fine-tuning your AI models. Proper planning ensures AI accurately understands customer inquiries, providing a positive user experience while meeting business objectives. Real-world simulations in your PoC will help to identify issues and refine the AI system before deployment.

Overall, planning is a fundamental aspect of any AI deployment. It establishes a solid foundation, mitigates risks, and ensures proper resource allocation to increase the potential for a successful project outcome.

2 Define Your Business Goals

One of the central business goals of deploying AI in your contact center should be to optimize operational efficiency.

Business goals for contact centers should define the purpose and direction of customer-centric operations. They serve as a compass, guiding contact center strategies and initiatives. Business goals take on added significance when planning to implement AI in a contact center, with the opportunity to reshape your contact center operations and elevate customer interactions. These goals should align with your company's desire to enhance operational efficiency and reflect the broader industry trend toward seamless, personalized, and efficient customer service.

First and foremost, optimizing operational efficiency should be one of your central business goals for deploying AI in your contact center. Traditional contact centers often grapple with manual processes, inherent inefficiencies, longer customer wait times, and increased agent workload. By leveraging AI-driven solutions like chatbots and virtual assistants, routine inquiries and tasks can be automated, freeing up human agents to tackle more complex and high-value interactions. This has the potential to reduce handling times, increase first-call resolution (FCR) rates, and, ultimately, boost customer satisfaction.

Another central business goal should be achieving higher personalization in customer interactions. Customers seek tailored experiences that resonate with their preferences and history. AI can analyze vast amounts of customer data in real time to assist agents with context-rich insights about each customer. This empowers agents to address customer needs more effectively, anticipate concerns, and suggest relevant solutions, leading to personalized and impactful interaction.

Cost optimization is also a significant driving force behind the adoption of AI in contact centers. A migration from on-premises systems to cloud-based solutions inherently brings cost savings in terms of hardware maintenance, software updates, and scalability. AI-powered tools can further contribute to cost reduction by handling routine tasks, reducing agent idle time, and enabling efficient workforce management. With a more streamlined operational model, your company can allocate resources more strategically and channel savings toward innovation and growth.

Enhancing customer engagement and loyalty is another central business goal for implementing AI. Contact centers can gauge customer emotions in real-time by harnessing AI-driven sentiment analysis and speech recognition. This allows agents to tailor their responses accordingly, defusing potentially tense situations and leaving customers feeling understood and valued. Positive interactions can increase customer loyalty, word-of-mouth referrals, and a strong brand reputation.

Lastly, the competitive advantage that AI offers cannot be overlooked. As businesses across industries embrace AI-driven solutions, customers have come to expect a certain level of technological sophistication in their interactions. Integrating AI seamlessly into your contact center operations, you position your company as an industry leader responsive to evolving customer needs. This, in turn, can attract new customers, retain existing ones, and set the stage for continued growth and innovation.

3 Outline Your AI Technology Goals

Your foremost technical goal should be seamlessly integrating AI solutions into your existing contact center infrastructure.

Outlining your AI technology goals for integrating AI into contact centers is essential for successfully deploying AI. When achieved, these goals should aim to harness the full potential of AI technologies while maintaining operational reliability and scalability.

Your foremost technical goal should be seamlessly integrating your AI solutions into your existing contact center infrastructure. This goal involves ensuring compatibility with existing systems, databases, and communication channels to minimize service disruptions when integrating your AI components. This goal should include a design for redundancy and failover mechanisms to ensure maximum uptime and availability in the event of hardware or software failures. This also includes developing mechanisms for incident response plans to address data breaches or security incidents with procedures for notifying affected parties and regulatory authorities if necessary.

High-quality data is the lifeblood of AI and vital for reliable decision-making and AI-driven insights. Plan to develop methods and procedures to ensure your data is accurate, consistent, and secure. Outline a plan for ingesting structured and unstructured data sources. Include scrubbing processes to check for typos, missing values, duplicates, outliers, and data inconsistencies. Propose data validation routines or implement automated data cleansing to detect and clean erroneous or inconsistent data with thresholds for acceptable data quality and flags for when data falls below your standards. Then, set goals for continuous improvement and model optimization using a data governance framework that includes data ownership, stewardship, and lifecycle management.

Contact centers handle sensitive customer data, making security and privacy paramount, and it's important to have technical measures like encryption, access controls, and anonymization in place. Plan to implement data auditing processes and logging mechanisms to track who accesses data and when, which can help identify potential security breaches. Include compliance with the General Data Protection Regulation (GDPR) and Health Insurance Portability and Accountability Act (HIPAA) regulations for data protection. Apply data masking and anonymization techniques to hide or replace sensitive information in datasets, making it difficult for unauthorized users to identify individuals.

AI applications in contact centers require real-time processing, such as natural language understanding, sentiment analysis, and call routing. Achieving low-latency responses in your network is critical to delivering timely and context-aware customer service. Implementing AI necessitates comprehensive monitoring and analytics capabilities. Plan to architect a technical infrastructure that enables real-time monitoring of AI systems for performance, accuracy, and security, and the ability to extract actionable insights from AI-generated data.

Technical training is a cornerstone of successful AI implementation, equipping your personnel with the knowledge and expertise to navigate AI tools and systems effectively. Technical training includes understanding AI algorithms, data preprocessing, model training, and ongoing maintenance. It also covers training for troubleshooting common issues, monitoring your Key Performance Indicators (KPIs), and how to review results for bias and accuracy.

These goals not only facilitate the adoption of AI but also ensure its sustainability and effectiveness in the long run. By achieving these technical goals and leveraging the power of AI in your contact center operations, your business can improve efficiency, enhance customer experiences, and remain competitive.

4 Understand AI Terminology

Artificial Intelligence and Generative AI both share the same parentage but represent distinct paradigms that chart divergent paths. Artificial General Intelligence will potentially perform any intellectual task a human can.

Artificial Intelligence, commonly called AI, is in the news with two terms often appearing at the forefront: AI and Generative AI (GAI). While they both fall under the expansive umbrella of artificial intelligence and share the same parentage, it is vital to grasp their nuances.

AI can be further categorized into narrow AI and strong AI. Narrow AI, or weak AI, is designed for a specific task or set of functions. Most of what is being labeled as AI today should be categorized as narrow AI, operating under a limited, predefined scope that does not possess general intelligence. However, narrow AI solutions are still considered powerful and complex, supporting applications like home virtual assistants such as Siri and Alexa or commercial chatbots. They just rely on human programming and training.

GAI systems are designed to produce output based on more than just pre-existing data. GAI can create original content. It goes beyond narrow task-specific AI and aims to achieve general problem-solving abilities across various domains. GAI evolved from ML and enables the ability to understand, learn, and apply knowledge across various tasks similar to humans. For contact centers, GAI solutions can be used to automate tasks such as answering frequently asked questions, routing calls to the appropriate agent, and providing personalized recommendations to customers.

Strong AI, commonly called Artificial General Intelligence (AGI), represents a theoretical form of AI that proposes solving any number of hypothetical tasks using generalized human cognitive abilities. In theory, AGI will be able to understand, learn, and apply knowledge across a wide range of functions, similar to humans. The ultimate goal of AGI is to replicate the broad range of human cognitive abilities called common-sense reasoning. AGI research is still evolving, and researchers are divided on the approach and timelines to bring it to reality.

Each category of AI represents distinct paradigms with varying capabilities. AI is the analytical powerhouse, harnessing data and algorithms to simulate human reasoning. GAI is the imaginative counterpart, conjuring novel content and artistic creations. AGI mimics human-like consciousness instead of simulating it, eventually teaching itself to solve new problems.

The distinction between AI and GAI becomes particularly pronounced in their applications. AI excels in tasks that demand pattern recognition and prediction. It's the force behind recommendation systems on streaming platforms and the brains of technologies such as self-driving cars. Generative AI, however, thrives in creative endeavors, generating content for customer communications, addressing their inquiries, guiding them through processes, and providing information.

AI and GAI can be pivotal in planning your contact center paradigm shift. AI can optimize call routing, analyze customer sentiments, and streamline operations, enhancing customer experience. GAI can revolutionize customer interactions. However, it's important to note that while GAI can improve the efficiency and effectiveness of contact centers, it may not be suitable for handling all types of interactions. Some complex or sensitive issues may still require human intervention. Therefore, you will need to plan a well-designed contact center strategy that often combines GAI with human agents to provide the best possible customer experience.

5 Plan What AI Technologies to Use

Planning for technical innovation is fluid. Technology evolves, and the only constant is change.

Prior to implementing AI, compare the different AI technologies available to meet your business and technical goals. AI is a broad field of computer science originating in the 1950s for developing systems that typically require human intelligence, such as problem-solving, reasoning, learning, perception, language understanding, and emotional intelligence. AI technologies encompass a range of capabilities, each with unique applications and benefits. Understanding the different types of AI that can be used in your contact center is essential for optimizing customer interactions and streamlining operations.

ML is a subset of AI developed in the 1980s to enable machines to learn from data, improve performance, and make decisions without explicit programming. ML algorithms encompass a variety of techniques, including supervised learning, unsupervised learning, and reinforcement learning. Supervised ML algorithms can be employed for sentiment analysis, allowing contact centers to gauge customer emotions during interactions. Unsupervised ML techniques aid in clustering customer data to identify patterns and preferences, enabling more personalized recommendations and targeted marketing. Reinforcement learning can optimize agent scheduling and resource allocation to enhance overall efficiency.

Generative AI (GAI) evolved from ML and enables human-like intelligence with the ability to understand, learn, and apply knowledge across a wide range of tasks similar to humans. GAI goes beyond task-specific narrow AI and aims to achieve general problem-solving abilities across various domains. It can autonomously manage a comprehensive range of customer interactions in contact centers, from answering queries to troubleshooting complex issues, without human intervention. Additionally, GAI has the capability to learn and adapt from each interaction in real time, thereby continually refining its algorithms to improve both operational efficiency and customer satisfaction.

Natural Language Processing, or NLP, can play a pivotal role in contact centers by enabling machines to understand, interpret, and generate human language. Chatbots and virtual agents equipped with NLP capabilities can engage in natural conversations with customers, offering quick and accurate responses to their inquiries. These AI-powered chatbots can assist with routine tasks, such as answering frequently asked questions, routing calls, or scheduling appointments, freeing human agents for more complex interactions.

Natural Language Understanding (NLU) encompasses speech recognition and Speech-Language Interpretation (SLU) to transform customer spoken words into text. Combined with NLG, these AI technologies' responses allow customers to interact in two-way conversations between the customer and your AI solution. Sentiment Analysis involves AI to assess the emotional tone of customer interactions so that contact centers can swiftly identify customer dissatisfaction or frustration.

Data analytics and big data empower contact centers to harness the vast amounts of data generated by customer interactions. AI-driven data analytics can extract valuable insights from call data records, enabling contact centers to make data-informed decisions, optimize processes, and identify areas for improvement.

These diverse types of AI offer the potential for a multitude of benefits, and it is essential for your planning to assess your specific needs and objectives when selecting and implementing these AI solutions to ensure they align with your broader goals and the evolving expectations of your customers.

6 The Essence of GAI and GAN

GAI provides the ability to generate original content, while Generative Adversarial Networks (GAN) give AI imagination.

The essence of GAI lies in its ability to generate new content that isn't explicitly programmed. This innovation arises from two main techniques: variational autoencoders and generative adversarial networks (GANs). Variational autoencoders allow machines to learn representations of data and then generate new data points based on those learned representations. On the other hand, GANs use two neural networks, the generator and the discriminator, which compete against each other.

In short, the generator's job is to fool the discriminator by generating samples close to the original content. The discriminator's job is to identify whether the generated sample is real or fake by comparing it to the original content. This tug-of-war leads to an iterative process where the generator becomes increasingly proficient at crafting convincing content.

GANs give AI systems something akin to imagination, making them less reliant on humans training them on your contact center operations. Without GAN, AI programmers need to be very explicit about what is included in the training data. This limits the effectiveness of your AI system and incurs high costs and labor. For planning, expect to use GAN to improve semi-supervised and unsupervised training, to ingest raw data, and to comprehend what is accurate and what is not.

A practical example of GAN is creating after-call work (ACW) summations using data collected from ACW summaries created by human agents. These summaries should cover key attributes such as the nature of the call, actions taken, resolutions, and any follow-up required. Plan to annotate the data to ensure its categorized and labeled attributes. The next step is training the GAN on the prepared dataset using a generator and a discriminator. The GAN generator learns to generate ACW summaries based on the input data by mimicking human-generated summaries' style and content. The GAN discriminator assesses the generated summaries and provides feedback to the generator, helping it improve over time.

Fine-tune the GAN to ensure that the generated summaries meet your specific quality criteria, refining the GAN's architecture and adjusting hyperparameters. Then, evaluate the GAN's performance using coherence, accuracy, and relevance metrics to assess how well it generates after-call work summaries. Over time, GAN fine-tuning can provide specific nuances and consistency in summary style.

It's worth noting that human oversight and verification may still be necessary, especially for complex or sensitive interactions. Additionally, the success of this approach depends on the quality of the training data and the continuous refinement of the GAN model.

Plan to look at both GANs and Large Language Models (LLM) for your AI-powered contact center. While GANs are known for generating creative content, LLMs are known for state-of-the-art NLP, answering questions, and creative writing. Nevertheless, GANs offer advantages for NLP, such as generating large amounts of high-quality and diverse data to augment LLMs. GANs can also capture complex and subtle features of natural language for both semantic coherence and grammatical correctness of language, such as style, tone, emotion, humor, and sarcasm, which can improve the naturalness and expressiveness of generated text and speech.

7 Generative AI Will Transform Customer Service

GAI can analyze your customer sentiment in real time. By monitoring language tone and cues, GAI can detect when a customer is becoming frustrated or dissatisfied.

Generative AI, or GAI, is poised to transform customer service in contact centers by offering powerful toolkits for enhancing efficiency, personalization, and overall customer satisfaction. Planning for this technology stack requires careful preparation, integration, and ongoing monitoring to ensure the technology aligns with your business goals and objectives.

Your businesses may already be using conversational AI chatbots to provide answers to customer questions. The next step is to transition to GAI, which allows chatbots to engage in entire conversations with your customers or provide transcripts of customers' conversations with your contact center agents. Additionally, suppose you are dealing with a diverse customer base. In that case, GAI can provide instant multilingual support by translating customer inquiries and responses, breaking down language barriers, and expanding the reach of your contact center.

GAI can assist customer service agents by analyzing historical data and customer interactions. Agent assist can suggest responses, recommend relevant information, and even provide real-time language translation by understanding natural language. GAI can accurately interpret customer queries and issues to support agent assist, analyze and categorize incoming requests, and then direct customers to the most appropriate agents or automated systems. Customer awareness-identified GAI can personalize responses to each caller, providing a personal touch that can improve customer experience and loyalty. GAI can also analyze your customer sentiment in real time. By monitoring language tone and cues, GAI can detect when a customer is becoming frustrated or dissatisfied. This enables timely intervention by escalating the issue to a human agent or offering a special promotion to appease the customer.

GAI automation can handle routine and repetitive tasks, such as answering frequently asked questions or processing standard requests. This frees human agents to focus on more complex and emotionally sensitive interactions, where human expertise is most valuable. Unlike human agents, GAI operates 24/7 without experiencing fatigue. This means customers can receive assistance at any time, ensuring that their issues and inquiries are addressed promptly. The availability around the clock is especially beneficial for businesses that cater to customers in different time zones. Automating routine tasks can also yield significant cost savings, allowing your business to reduce operational costs by optimizing your workforce schedules.

As GAI performs these tasks, it generates a wealth of data that can be invaluable for decision-making. The data provides insights into customer behavior, preferences, and pain points and can be the foundation of strategic decisions, allowing your business to tailor your services to meet customer needs effectively. The data will also enable GAI to learn from interactions, adapting and improving continually. As your contact center handles increased queries and gathers more data, the AI becomes increasingly proficient at providing accurate and helpful responses.

GAI has immense potential to transform contact center customer service. It offers many benefits, from enhancing agent support and personalizing responses to automating tasks and providing 24/7 availability. However, successful implementation requires careful planning, integration, and ongoing monitoring to ensure that GAI aligns with your contact center's specific objectives and key results.

8 Select Your AI Domains

Understanding the specific capabilities and functions of different AI domains is essential for making informed decisions to select the right tools and technologies.

In planning for AI in your contact center, it is vital to thoughtfully select the most appropriate domains that align with your contact center's strategic objectives and operational needs. Before adopting AI technologies, assess your existing technological ecosystem to identify any potential bottlenecks or compatibility issues. In addition, ensure you have high-quality and sufficient data to support your chosen AI domain.

As you plan your AI-powered contact center, several AI domains may be relevant, with each domain offering unique capabilities that can be tailored to address specific challenges and goals within the contact center environment. For example, multiple domains may exist for your customers interacting with your AI solution.

On the surface, the domain of natural language processing, or NLP, and the domain of conversational AI may appear the same. However, NLP focuses on understanding, interpreting, and manipulating human language by computers and deals with processing text and speech data between computers and your customers. Conversational AI involves AI-driven chatbots and virtual assistants capable of natural and dynamic conversations. NLP and Conversational AI are related but distinct domains. NLP is a foundational technology for understanding and processing language; conversational AI extends beyond NLP to create interactive, human-like conversations between machines and users.

Speech Recognition, also known as Automatic Speech Recognition (ASR), is another domain for accurately converting or transcribing spoken language into written text. The main difference between the NLP domain and the Speech Recognition domain lies in the type of input data they handle. NLP deals with text-based language understanding and generation, while Speech Recognition is dedicated to converting spoken language into written text. Sentiment analysis is another distinct domain that analyzes text or speech to determine the emotional tone or sentiment expressed and helps gauge customer satisfaction and identify potential issues.

Machine Learning, or ML, is a broader domain of various algorithms and techniques for making predictions and decisions based on data. ML can be applied in contact centers for predictive analytics, customer segmentation, and fraud detection. Two subfields of ML are the domains of deep learning and reinforcement learning. The deep learning domain uses neural networks with multiple layers to analyze and make decisions from complex data. It's used in applications like speech recognition, image analysis, and chatbot development. The domain for reinforcement learning focuses on developing algorithms and models that enable virtual agents to learn how to make decisions by interacting with your AI environment. Unlike supervised learning, where models are trained on labeled data, and unsupervised learning, which involves finding patterns in unlabeled data, reinforcement learning involves learning from trial and error. Predictive analytics is another domain that uses historical data and statistical algorithms to predict future events or trends, such as forecasting call volumes, customer behavior, and resource planning.

Understanding the specific capabilities and functions of different AI domains is essential for making informed decisions in your plan to select the right tools and technologies that align with your contact center's goals and requirements.

9 Detail Your AI Domain Descriptions

AI Domain Descriptions are detailed explanations or specifications of the specific AI domains and refer to particular areas or fields of knowledge.

Deploying AI/ML solutions within a specific domain description requires a deep understanding of the domain's operational landscape. AI/ML technology vendors may not have the expertise to guide you through implementing AI in your contact center. Consider using an expert with the proficiency to perform iterative improvements. Insight from these performance loops will ensure your AI/ML solutions remain relevant and effective in addressing the evolving challenges of the domain.

Distinguish between the terms "AI Domain" and "AI Domain Descriptions." AI Domain typically refers to a broad category or area of expertise within artificial intelligence. It encompasses the various fields, techniques, and technologies related to AI-driven capabilities. For example, NLP, ML, sentiment analysis, reinforcement learning, and speech recognition are different AI domains.

On the other hand, AI Domain Descriptions are detailed explanations or specifications of the specific AI domains and refer to particular areas or fields of knowledge where AI techniques and technologies are applied to solve certain problems or address specific challenges. These descriptions provide a deeper understanding of the AI technologies, their applications, and how they fit into your contact center setup. Domain descriptions could include information about the capabilities of AI technologies within the chosen domain, their benefits, potential use cases, and considerations for implementation as well as define the scope and context of your AI application.

Experts can provide insights into what you will need in your AI/ML solution and help identify potential challenges, roadblocks, or opportunities for optimization during deployment. AI domain description expertise for your business area should be foundational in selecting your AI/ML vendor. The vendor's domain experience integrating AI/ML into your specific domain is vital to a successful solution. Moreover, domain descriptions are dynamic and subject to change over time due to evolving technologies, trends, and external factors. For instance, if you're focused on the NLP domain, your AI domain description would include:

- Core concepts within NLP for text analysis, language understanding, and language generation
- Technology description and techniques commonly used in NLP, including tokenization, part-of-speech tagging, and sentiment analysis
- Real-world applications of NLP in contact centers, such as chatbots for customer support, automated email responses, or analyzing customer feedback
- The benefits and advantages of NLP in a contact center setting, including improved customer interactions, faster query resolution, and enhanced customer satisfaction
- Potential challenges and limitations, like handling multilingual support or addressing privacy concerns when processing customer data
- Insights to implement NLP within a contact center, including data requirements, integration with existing systems, and best practices
- Use cases demonstrating how NLP has been successfully deployed in contact centers to solve specific problems or enhance operations

Ensure the vendor's AI domain description experts are positioned to continuously refine and improve your AI/ML models as new data becomes available and the domain evolves. Weigh each vendor's ability to detect shifts in patterns, trends, or anomalies that might impact your model's performance.

10 Outline Your AI Project Lifecycle

AI project lifecycle will help identify the necessary details to meet your AI goals and maintain effective control of your project.

Knowing the steps required for project execution is important regardless of what you do, but it is especially vital when it comes to AI solutions. Understanding an AI project lifecycle will help identify the details needing attention if your goals include AI. Implementing AI in a contact center environment requires careful planning and a well-defined overall plan. This includes gathering information about your business goals and what resources are needed at each step. Ultimately, this translates into maintaining control of the project more effectively.

AI may be intriguing to pursue as a cool state-of-the-art technology. However, it's crucial to remember that AI should only be deployed when there's an actual necessity. AI projects should be motivated by a genuine problem or objective. It's important to understand that AI isn't always necessary to achieve your desired outcome. Determine if your goals can be achieved with simpler solutions or if your objectives really require more complex resources like AI.

The first lifecycle stage ensures that the deployment of AI in the contact center aligns with the organization's overarching business objectives. By establishing clear goals and defining the desired outcomes, the plan enables the contact center to focus on the specific areas where AI can drive the most value, such as improving customer satisfaction, increasing efficiency, or reducing operational costs.

The second lifecycle stage involves planning for significant investments in technology, infrastructure, and training. An overall plan helps identify and allocate the necessary resources, whether budgetary considerations, personnel training, or infrastructure upgrades. This ensures your business is prepared to support an AI deployment effectively.

The third lifecycle stage involves technology evaluation and integration. Contact center ecosystems comprise various systems and processes that need to integrate with AI technologies seamlessly. An overall plan facilitates evaluating different AI solutions, selecting the most suitable ones, and ensuring their successful integration with existing systems. It also helps avoid fragmented implementations and provides a cohesive AI ecosystem within the contact center.

Planning to introduce AI in the contact center represents a substantial change for management, operational staff, and agents. An overall plan allows for proper change management, including training and communication strategies. It helps address concerns, provide support, and ensure the workforce is equipped with the necessary skills to collaborate effectively with AI systems.

Contact center AI comes with its own risks and challenges, such as data privacy, security breaches, and ethical considerations. Having an overarching plan allows businesses to anticipate potential risks, plan necessary safeguards, and ensure compliance with regulatory requirements. Note that emerging data privacy standards may dictate the level of AI or ML tools access. Planning includes establishing policies and guidelines for responsible AI usage, ensuring customer trust, and mitigating potential reputational or legal risks. It should also entail defining Key Performance Indicators, known as KPIs, and establishing mechanisms for monitoring and evaluating the impact of AI in the contact center. KPIs enable businesses to measure the effectiveness of an AI implementation, identify areas for improvement, and iterate on the deployment strategy. Continuous monitoring and improvement help maximize the benefits derived from AI and ensure its long-term success.

11 Plan Your Technology Sequence of Actions

Whatever your objectives, your plan needs to begin with thoroughly assessing your existing ecosystem.

The migration of a contact center from an on-premises telephony solution to the cloud while implementing AI and GAI is a multifaceted process that demands careful planning and execution. This transition represents a pivotal shift in how your contact centers will operate, leveraging cloud technologies and advanced AI capabilities to enhance customer interactions, streamline operations, and drive efficiencies. Integration is always a key challenge in any migration, and your AI solutions should seamlessly integrate with your existing ecosystem. Objectives for your migration can vary widely and may include cost reduction, scalability, improved customer service, real-time analytics, and the integration of AI-powered capabilities to enhance customer experiences.

Whatever the objectives, your plan needs to begin with a thorough assessment of your existing Private Branch eXchange (PBX), Auto Call Distribution (ACD), Interactive Voice Response (IVR), dialer, voice/screen recording systems, and supporting adjunct components. This includes documenting all hardware, software, configurations, and their interdependencies. Understanding the current state is fundamental to crafting a migration plan that mitigates risks and preserves critical functionality.

Choosing the right AI technology is also a pivotal decision. Factors such as reliability, security, scalability, and the entirety of AI capabilities must be considered. Cloud providers, including AWS, Azure, and Google Cloud, offer comprehensive AI environments well-suited for contact centers. While these cloud providers provide complete solutions for contact centers, Contact Center as a Service (CCaaS) vendors also use cloud providers to offer competitive solutions. Your planning should evaluate all vendors and compare features and functionality.

Plan for data and application migration to transfer data and contact center applications, such as customer relationship management (CRM), to the cloud environment. This should encompass customer data, voice recordings, call records, and relevant software. This will require meticulous planning and testing, which is essential to ensure data integrity and functionality post-migration.

On-premise systems may involve multiple servers in a tightly coupled architecture. For example, in some environments, each product may reside on one or more virtual or physical computers. Your systems may be configured as high availability to ensure your business is always operational. Plan to include any adjunct components and applications from your PBX that may provide operational support. For instance, you may support robust reporting for operations or for Enhanced 911 to comply with Kari's Law and Ray Baum's Act.

Migration of toll-free numbers (TFN) and direct inward dialing (DID) also requires planning. Many CCaaS vendors offer TFNs and DIDs from their telecommunications carriers. In some cases, CCaaS vendors maintain a carrier hotel with multiple telecommunication carriers in their data centers. Review the base cost and cost per minute from the CCaaS vendors and compare them to your expenses. There are advantages to having your carrier connect to the CCaaS vendors in what is known as Bring Your Own Carrier (BYOC). One of the benefits of BYOC may be better pricing. Another is direct control over your numbers. Many carriers offer the ability to distribute your call volume by percentage to different locations. Using the ability to distribute calls by percentages enables you to plan a gradual migration to a cloud solution while maintaining your existing telephony components.

12 Plan Your Sequence of Actions for Business

Your business and technical team should mutually agree on what needs to be accomplished.

When planning your sequence of action for business, aligning it with your technical actions is essential. Your business and technical team should mutually agree on what needs to be accomplished, like cost savings, scalability, improved performance, or enhanced customer experience. Establish a timeline for implementing AI in your contact center, taking into account any organizational roadblocks or budget limitations.

Plan to be transparent with your customers during the migration to AI. Effective communication with your customers is fundamental throughout the migration. Inform your customers about the changes and provide clear instructions for using new features or channels. Communication will give a positive customer experience during the transition and help gain customer acceptance of the AI solution.

Your business operational procedures and historical knowledge base are vital to identifying the data to model, train, and test the system. After your AI system is live, your business needs to be involved in ongoing refinement and optimization of your AI models. Continuous learning is crucial to improving the accuracy of your data models and enhancing the overall customer experience. Plan to leverage the scalability of a cloud environment to accommodate fluctuations in call volumes and business requirements to ensure your AI solutions can adapt and scale with your contact center's evolving needs.

Training contact center staff on effectively using available AI tools is equally important. Your business staff must be well-equipped to leverage the new cloud-based systems and AI tools. Providing comprehensive training and ongoing support is necessary to maximize the benefits of these technologies.

Plan for a gradual transition from your on-premise system to a cloud-based solution. This phase requires careful oversight to address issues and ensure a smooth transition. Set up robust monitoring and analytics tools to track the performance of the contact center and AI systems in real time. Data-driven insights are invaluable for making informed decisions and optimizing operations. Plan to develop cost management strategies to control cloud-related expenses. This includes planning to monitor resource utilization and optimizing cloud resources to align with the actual needs of the contact center.

Security considerations are paramount. In addition to implementing robust security measures, including encryption, access controls, and data protection mechanisms, compliance is essential to safeguard customer data and conform with industry regulations and privacy laws.

Plan to create and maintain detailed documentation of the cloud architecture, AI models, and configurations for future reference and troubleshooting. Knowledge transfer within the organization ensures that staff are well-equipped to manage and maintain the new environment.

After the migration, plan for your business to comprehensively evaluate the new setup. Gather feedback from employees and customers to identify areas for improvement and fine-tuning. Plan to stay proactive by keeping abreast of advancements in AI and cloud technologies. As AI technology advances, it's vital for both your business and technical teams to remain coordinated to stay competitive and consistently provide the experience your customers expect.

13 Assess Your Contact Center

Begin your assessment with the core of your operation and customer interactions. If the majority of your customer interactions are straightforward, there is an opportunity for automation.

As part of your strategy planning, assess the various aspects of your contact center operations, technology, and performance. Use a high-level methodology to define your objectives from the assessment. A methodology will establish the necessary foundational requirements for AI in your contact center.

Begin with the core of your operation: customer interactions. What kind of questions do customers frequently ask? Are these queries repetitive and straightforward, or do they often require nuanced understanding and problem-solving? AI excels at handling repetitive tasks. If the majority of your customer interactions are straightforward, then there is an opportunity for automation.

Analyze your data volume and complexity. Simply put, the more data you have, the better AI will perform. Pay attention to call handling procedures, escalation protocols, response times, and customer service scripts. Review call logs, customer interaction histories, agent skills, and performance metrics such as average handle time (AHT), average speed of answer (ASA), and ACW.

However, this is about more than just the amount of data. Complex data is multi-dimensional and may include purchase history, interaction logs, voice recordings, and social media. It allows AI systems to understand context, make predictions, and offer more personalized solutions. For instance, an AI system trained on complex data could identify a valued customer with past issues and instantly route them to a senior agent while providing that agent with a detailed customer profile. Your analysis should balance both volume and complexity. High volume gives your AI the raw material it needs, while complexity provides the nuances, allowing intelligent decision-making.

Consider the human element of your contact center and their role in an AI-powered contact center. Agents bring something AI can't, such as empathy, creativity, and the ability to think outside the box. At the same time, agents need to be somewhat tech-savvy to work alongside AI tools. Assess the skill set of your human agents. Will they need training? Can they shift to roles that require more complex problem-solving, leaving routine tasks to AI?

If the contact center supports multi-channel capabilities like phone, email, live chat, and social media, assess their effectiveness and consistency to ensure your customers have a seamless and unified experience across all channels. Plan your AI solution to have similar capabilities to maintain the context and intent across all channels.

Efficient inbound contact centers are the backbone of excellent phone support; metrics help maximize their performance. Review your key performance indicators, including first call resolution (FCR) rate, average handling time, customer satisfaction (CSAT) scores, agent performance metrics, service level agreements (SLA), and quality monitoring results. Gauging the customer experience is especially true when planning chatbots and conversational AI. Plan to maintain or improve your AI solution's key performance indicators (KPI).

Verify that the contact center complies with industry regulations and internal security protocols. This is crucial, primarily if sensitive customer data is handled. Your AI solution must comply with your industry's regulations, the privacy of your customers' information, and overall security.

14 Understand Your Business Objectives

AI projects should be motivated by a genuine problem or objective. It's important to understand that AI isn't always necessary to achieve your desired outcome.

AI may be intriguing to pursue as a state-of-the-art technology. Yet, it's crucial to remember that AI should only be deployed when there's an actual purpose. AI projects should be motivated by a genuine problem or objective. It's important to understand that AI isn't always necessary to achieve your desired outcome. Determine if your goals can be achieved with more straightforward solutions or if your objectives require more complex resources like AI. When developing an AI plan for a contact center, defining the business objectives and goals that AI implementation aims to achieve is essential.

Customers have two priorities: quickly solving their problems and working with someone skilled in resolving them. This presents a conflict between what customers expect and what they experience, which you will need to address. Past attempts to introduce entirely virtual agents inevitably failed for numerous reasons, mainly because they didn't sound human or were not programmed to answer customer inquiries. Calls answered by virtual agents with a robotic voice saying, "Hello, I am an AI agent. How may I help you?" may be promptly met with an abrupt customer response of "AGENT!"

This is no longer the case. With the pace of AI advancement, virtual agents are able to communicate in a natural voice, language, and rhythm, fully understand context, interpret customer data, and solve problems with empathy that mimics human qualities. In essence, these new virtual agents are nearly indistinguishable from humans when conversing over the phone and provide help better and faster than humans.

If your objective is to increase operational efficiency, AI can automate repetitive tasks, such as call routing and completing form-based data. This can free agents to focus on more complex tasks, such as intricate problem-solving or customer-escalated interactions. AI-powered software can also analyze sentiment to track your customers' reactions and emotions in real time. To illustrate, a frustrated customer might pause more often, or their tone of voice may go up. AI can pick up on these signals by analyzing the tone and cadence of a phone call. AI offers live agent feedback via pop-up messages so that the agent can respond appropriately to their customer's needs.

Contact centers are notoriously challenging places to work. Agent turnover is high, and the jobs are stressful. As such, agents may feel optimistic about AI supporting them at work. AI can help contact center agents perform better by providing real-time assistance, suggesting responses, and next-best-action recommendations for agents to provide more personalized and effective customer support.

With the proper planning and preparation, your AI-powered contact center can achieve your business objectives and goals, including improving customer satisfaction, increasing operational efficiency, reducing costs, enhancing agent performance, optimizing customer support, improving call center performance metrics, and enhancing data management. By defining clear business objectives and goals, your contact center can realize a comprehensive AI that aligns with your business objectives, enhances your customer experience, and maximizes the benefits of AI technology.

15 Understand Your Costs

It is essential to understand your contact center costs. Without an audit of costs, any efforts to introduce AI may be at odds with your business goals. Contact centers have six major cost drivers: call volume, agent handle time, labor costs, technology and infrastructure costs, training and development costs, and facilities costs.

Call volume is the number of inbound and outbound calls for voice and fax telecommunications and Short Messaging Services (SMS). Telecommunication costs are determined by the number of channels and the cost per minute carriers charge, specifically for TFNs. If you are using Session Initiation Protocol (SIP), there is also a cost for Concurrent Call Paths (CCP) on the SIP trunks. Telecommunication costs are not likely to vary unless your goal is to redirect your calls to web chat, email, or social media. In this case, you will need to determine the costs for internet bandwidth.

Agent handle time, referred to as AHT, is the time to complete a customer inquiry plus the ACW time. Longer AHT requires more staff to minimize customer time in queue. Since labor cost is the most significant expense in a contact center operation, reducing the AHT by just a few seconds per transaction translates into high cost and performance benefits.

Labor costs include salaries, wages, and benefits. Total labor costs are determined by knowing the number of agents needed for an optimum staffing level to cover your operating hours. Understaffing will reduce payroll but result in poor service. Overstaffing will increase the payroll but may not improve performance. Workforce Management (WFM) systems can optimize staffing models that support lower labor costs.

Technology and infrastructure costs depend on various technologies and infrastructure components to support call center software, CRM systems, IVR systems, ACD systems, adjunct telephony servers, and network infrastructure. General maintenance and keeping version levels current can add these costs to your bottom line.

Investing in the training and development of contact center agents is essential for providing high-quality customer service. Training and development costs include programs to cover product knowledge, communication skills, soft skills, compliance, and other areas to improve agent performance. Continuous training and development contribute to agent retention and better customer satisfaction but also add to the contact center's operating expenses. Plan for this expense to increase with the introduction of new AI-powered tools.

Real estate and facilities costs include the physical space needed to accommodate contact center personnel, rent, utilities, and maintenance expenses. Before the pandemic, contact centers were large operations with numerous agents. Optimizing the use of space and considering cost-effective locations were principles for managing this expense. However, many organizations now support work-at-home agents, which has allowed organizations to downsize the square footage of their facilities.

To obtain your goals and objectives, it is vital to create a budget proposal that considers the effects of AI in all relevant categories, including known and unknown factors.

16 Separate ACD and IVR Functionality

ACDs and IVRs are often confused and used interchangeably.

Contact center processes are businesses with structured procedures to manage customer interactions across multiple communication channels. Automatic Call Distributors, called ACD systems, are telephony systems that distribute incoming calls to the most available or best-skilled contact center agents or representatives. An ACD can determine a customer's intent through programmed call flows and connect them to a skilled agent. Traditional IVRs also use structured programmed call flows to assess the customer's intent.

Thus, ACDs and IVRs are often confused and used interchangeably. Both provide structured call flows for customers to interact and determine the type of assistance requested before they queue to an agent. One difference is that IVRs can access CRM systems to personalize customer interaction. They can also perform ASR and Text-To-Speech (TTS) to handle the customer's queries without agent intervention. In contrast, an ACD only performs call routing based on decision tree logic to connect callers with an appropriately skilled agent.

Modern ACDs can prompt customers with prerecorded recordings and collect digits for scripted options. To illustrate, most callers have experienced a telephony system saying, "Press 1 for option a, press 2 for option b." ACDs operate solely on the response from the caller. It cannot access external systems to personalize the interaction.

Voice circuits must be terminated at an on-premises ACD, which manages the call during the entirety of the customer interaction. Inbound calls are answered by an ACD and then transferred to an IVR when personalized interactions are desired. After the customer interacts with the IVR, the call is transferred back to the ACD, which may check agent availability based on the time of day and holiday schedules. If agents are available, the call is placed in a queue to be answered in sequence. Outbound calls initiated by a dialer are also managed by the ACD. When programmed, customers may answer the phone, listen to a message, and request the transfer to an agent or a bot to complete an interaction.

As you plan a migration to AI, consider that the ACD can remain on-premises. Instead of transferring the call to an IVR, the call can be directed to a cloud-based conversational AI system. The AI system can understand what is asked and generate a suitable response within the context of a conversation. This is similar to an IVR but more sophisticated. AI can accomplish this through mathematical logic to interpret user input, generate appropriate responses, and maintain the coherence and flow of the conversation. If the AI completes the customer's interaction, the call ends. If the AI system needs to escalate to an agent, the AI system transfers the call back to the ACD with the customer's intent. Using the customer intent, the ACD queues the call to the most appropriate skill or to an agent with the proper attributes to help the customer.

ACD also maintains call details. For instance, a call management system (CMS) is a comprehensive system that provides real-time and historical reporting on call center performance, agent productivity, and customer interactions, enabling supervisors and managers access to customizable dashboards, automated reporting, and agent performance tracking.

The ACD uniquely provides a telephony service application programming interface (TSAPI) allowing third-party applications to programmatically initiate, manage, and terminate calls. Third-party control provides functions to make outbound calls, answer incoming calls, put calls on hold, transfer calls, and end calls.

17 Consider AI for Call Routing

Traditional telephony systems for routing calls to agents have evolved over decades but remain on techniques found in the first switchboard patented in 1891 by Almon Brown Strowger and later acquired by Bell in 1916. The introduction of an automated switching system allowed people in La Porte, Indiana, to contact each other without the assistance of a telephone operator. The first ACD systems originated in the 1950s and made it possible to filter and route calls to the right agent at the right time using an algorithm to determine the best agent to receive each call. Through the 1970s and 1980s, technological advancements continued to improve call routing and the efficiency of servicing the customer. IVR systems interfaced with the ACD to add self-help options and qualify customers' needs for improved call routing. Additional systems have also been interfaced with the ACD for call history and third-party call control. More recently, contact centers have offered additional communication channels to customers, such as webchat and short messaging services (SMS). Today, the traditional ACD is a myriad of individual systems tightly coupled to form the contact center telephony system. In larger companies, the telephony infrastructure is complex and requires skilled engineers to administer and maintain the ecosystem.

AI introduces new options, and rather than append your AI solution to your traditional telephony infrastructure, consider AI as the core call routing system. AI has the potential to transform and perform many of the functions usually handled by ACDs, IVRs, Dialers, WFM, call recording, and call management systems in a monolithic application.

To illustrate this integrated approach, imagine a customer calling your business. AI-powered systems employ NLP and ASR technologies. Using voice analysis and speech patterns, the AI system determines the purpose of the call. AI algorithms immediately access and analyze data about the customer, including history and preferences; AI routing decisions take into account factors such as customer value, issue severity, sentiment analysis, agent availability, and language preferences to match the caller with the most suitable agent in the same manner as ACD attribute-based routing. One of the key features of AI call routing is its ability to make dynamic, real-time decisions by continuously evaluating incoming calls and agent availability and adjusting routing strategies as conditions change. One caution is that during busy periods, the AI system might prioritize routing calls to agents with relevant skills, even if they are currently engaged in other calls.

Throughout the call, AI analyzes data to gain insights into customer behavior, call patterns, and agent performance. These insights serve as the foundation for making intelligent routing decisions. The AI system monitors the performance of routing decisions, tracking metrics like call resolution times, customer satisfaction, and agent productivity, and assesses agent workload, availability, and performance, suggesting workload adjustments or breaks to maintain agent productivity and well-being. Feedback from these metrics is used to continuously refine and improve the routing algorithms, ensuring the system becomes increasingly effective and efficient over time.

18 Define Your AI-Powered Performance Indicators

AI performance indicators can reveal bottlenecks in processing, detect specific steps where delays occur, identify trends, monitor customer sentiment, and evaluate agent performance.

Performance indicators are the backbone of managing efficiencies in your contact center and can help provide insight into customer satisfaction and conversational AI performance. Ultimately, performance indicators tell you whether your AI-powered contact center or agent performance is healthy and on-target to meet your business goals.

In my book, *42 Rules for Using AI in Your Contact Center,* Rules 31 and 32, I outline the metrics used in AI-powered contact centers. By utilizing ML algorithms, AI-powered performance indicators can enhance your analytics of collected data points to identify trends, monitor customer sentiment, and evaluate agent performance. This data offers a more comprehensive comprehension of how customers interact, enhancing your overall customer satisfaction.

Your plan should outline how to utilize AI-powered analytics as part of any proposed contact center AI software package. The analytics software should have pre-built reports that align with your business goals. And agents should have access to real-time performance analytics, too. You'll need to plan ahead to get the most out of your software.

Plan what you want to achieve with AI. Is it improving customer satisfaction, reducing wait times, or something else? Align AI goals with overall business objectives. Identify your most important performance indicators, such as AHT, FCR, CSAT scores, or a combination of contact center AI metrics, including Interaction Handle Time (IHT). Ensure you can adjust the timeframes for data analysis to view trends over the past day, week, or month or compare data from different periods. Most AI analytics dashboards offer visualizations like charts and graphs. These help you quickly understand trends and patterns in the data. If you spot an interesting trend, plan for capabilities to drill down for more detailed information. For instance, if you see a spike in call volume, you can explore which times of day it occurred.

Plan to segment your data based on different parameters to analyze performance based on agent, team, customer demographics, or specific products/services. AI can highlight insights that might not be immediately obvious. For example, it might identify specific phrases that correlate with high customer satisfaction. Some AI analytics offer predictive capabilities. These can forecast future trends, helping you proactively adjust staffing or resources. AI-powered analytics performance indicators often provide real-time data with specific thresholds to alert and notify your teams. This is particularly useful for making immediate decisions, such as reallocating agents to handle a sudden increase in inquiries or understanding if AI conversational bots are not performing. AI analytics may also identify changes in your routing strategies. For example, if certain products generate above-average customer inquiries, consider creating a dedicated support channel for the product.

AI performance indicators can also reveal bottlenecks in processing, identifying specific steps where delays occur. Plan to compare the performance of AI interactions with human interactions to the effectiveness of AI in various scenarios. Integrate a feedback loop to provide insights into whether the AI analytic performance indicator aligns with agent performance.

19 Prepare for Data Collection

Data collection challenges may include computing resource costs, lack of skilled personnel, poor ML tools, or weak data governance issues.

"Data" is the term used to describe knowledge or information encoded in a way that enables it to be used effectively to enhance AI decision-making and the core of all AI/ML projects, from conversational voice bots to emotional recognition. Many organizations understand the importance of AI and its potential impact on their business, but they often struggle to move from pilot to production. For ML systems to recognize patterns and make decisions, AI must first be trained with data to recognize those patterns. This means that your plan must include large amounts of data for the algorithms to learn from.

Data collection challenges may include computing resource costs, lack of skilled personnel, poor ML tools, or weak data governance issues. However, the biggest challenge is ingesting data in large amounts of varied and high-quality data. Low-quality data can prolong moving your AI to a production state because your ML models will not function as intended and fail to deliver desired results.

Preparing for this challenge can be a formidable task. ML must be precise to be beneficial, and this can only be achieved with high-quality data. Plan to identify key data sources for intake, such as call logs, customer interactions, and sentiment data. To ensure success, your plan should consider a cloud infrastructure to manage the huge amount of data from high call volumes and real-time data intake. The design should be a flexible, intelligent infrastructure that needs minimal management so your business can handle large data volumes and process data, regardless of how many users there are.

Plan to assess the quality of data before collecting to ensure your ML model's success. Poor-quality data can introduce biases, leading to unfair and inaccurate outcomes. Evaluating your data for completeness, correctness, consistency, and relevance is essential. Incomplete or inconsistent data can misrepresent patterns and produce unreliable predictions. Incorrect data introduces noise that hinders model performance. Biased data perpetuates unfair predictions, adversely affecting certain groups. A rigorous data quality assessment guarantees robust AI models with enhanced generalization capabilities and mitigates potential ethical dilemmas. By prioritizing data quality, you can build AI systems that provide unbiased, accurate, and reliable results, fostering trust and confidence in AI applications.

To optimize your AI results, plan for a diverse range of data. Identify various types of data with multiple layers to improve the accuracy of your data models. For instance, basic demographic data only provides a general idea of a customer. Additional customer profiles may include marital status, education, employment, income, purchase history, and geographic location.

Collecting this data carries the responsibility of privacy and ethics. Prioritize compliance with data privacy regulations and ethical considerations to protect customers' rights and autonomy. Anonymizing or pseudonymizing data is one way to safeguard and ensure your customers' privacy. Plan for regular audits and assessments to help maintain compliance. Maintain the ethical principles of your business to safeguard fairness and non-discrimination and avoid biased outcomes.

Plan for adequate security measures to prevent unauthorized access or breaches. Transparency in data handling and providing clear privacy policies to your customers fosters trust. Plan for regular audits and assessments to help maintain compliance. Ethical principles, like fairness and non-discrimination, must guide data collection and processing, avoid biased outcomes, and respect individuals' autonomy.

20 Identify Your Data Sources

Primary data refers to data collected directly from customers and contact center operations. Secondary data refers to information collected from external sources.

Sourcing high-quality and diverse data is principal in planning effective and robust AI systems. Data serves as the foundation upon which AI algorithms learn, adapt, and make informed decisions. The process of sourcing data for AI involves meticulous collection, curation, and preparation of information from various sources, such as databases, sensors, social media platforms, and more. Ensuring data accuracy, relevance, and ethical considerations are essential steps in this journey. With the correct data, AI developers can empower their models to tackle complex problems, deliver innovative systems, and pave the way for transformative advancements across a wide range of industries. Therefore, the data for your AI solution must be not only of high quality but also relevant to the problem.

Sourcing primary and secondary data for contact centers involves gathering and utilizing information from different channels to improve customer service, enhance operational efficiency, and gain valuable insights for strategic decision-making.

Primary data refers to data collected directly from customers and contact center operations. This data can be obtained through various means, such as customer surveys, feedback forms, live chats, call recordings, and direct customer interactions during calls.

Secondary data refers to information collected from external sources. For contact centers, this may include industry reports, customer behavior trends, benchmarking data, and market analysis. Secondary data helps contact centers understand broader market trends, benchmark their performance against industry standards, and make data-driven decisions based on external insights.

Plan to clean your data by identifying and addressing data inconsistencies, such as removing duplicates, handling missing values, correcting errors, and standardizing formats. A clean dataset ensures that labeling efforts focus on relevant and meaningful data by eliminating noise and irrelevant information, leading to more accurate annotations.

After gathering and purifying your data, it's important to label it by identifying and marking data samples. Labeling is another step in NL that transforms raw data into meaningful information. Precise annotation of primary data from original sources and utilizing labeled secondary data from external sources help train your data-driven AI algorithms.

Primary data labeling involves the manual or automated annotation of data directly collected from original sources. This process often requires domain expertise and human involvement to tag and categorize data points accurately, such as images, texts, or audio, to create labeled datasets for training ML models.

Secondary data labeling involves using existing labeled datasets or external sources to supplement primary data. By leveraging pre-labeled data or external databases, data scientists can augment the training process, expand the scope of their models, and improve their algorithms' performance on diverse datasets. The combination of primary and secondary data labeling methodologies ensures the creation of comprehensive and high-quality datasets that enable contact centers to enhance their operations, optimize customer experiences, and make well-informed decisions to stay competitive and meet the evolving needs of their customers.

21 | Redact Your Data

Redaction helps maintain data integrity by ensuring that only pertinent information is included in the dataset.

Training your ML model requires data. Lots of data. Lots of quality data, to be precise. While data is the cornerstone for training robust and accurate AI models, it often contains confidential information that can be misused if exposed. Data redaction involves sanitizing or anonymizing data and removing or modifying specific pieces of information that could identify an individual or reveal sensitive details. Traditional methods of data redaction include data masking, pseudonymization, and anonymization. These techniques can replace the actual data with fictional but structurally similar data, map data to a random alias, or remove identifiers altogether.

However, before you can redact data, you need to identify what data is sensitive and needs to be protected. This could include personally identifiable information (PII), financial information, health information, or other confidential data. Also, identify and remove irrelevant data that can introduce noise and skew the AI model's learning process.

In a conventional centralized model, redaction helps maintain data integrity by ensuring that only pertinent information is included in the dataset. Traditional methods of data redaction include data masking, pseudonymization, and anonymization. Such techniques replace your actual data with fictional but structurally similar data, map data to a random alias, or remove identifiers altogether.

However, conventional methods of data redaction may only partially be suitable for federated learning scenarios, Federated learning scenarios offer enhanced data privacy, reduced data transfer overheads, real-time adaptability, and easier regulatory compliance, addressing critical limitations of traditional centralized data models in machine learning applications.

Federated learning often involves complex data structures and types requiring more granular control than traditional redaction methods. The data in federated systems is usually dynamic, updating in real-time, which requires redaction techniques that can adapt swiftly. Redaction must be performed in a way that does not add significant computational burdens to the system, defeating the purpose of decentralization. When redaction is implemented across various nodes, there needs to be a level of consistency that allows the model to learn effectively without bias by the redaction techniques employed at individual nodes.

Emerging ecosystems for these challenges are multifaceted. One approach is differential privacy, which adds noise to the data or queries in a way that the overall data distribution is maintained, but individual data points are obfuscated. Another option is homomorphic encryption, enabling mathematical operations on encrypted data, thus keeping the data secure while still useful for learning. Secure multi-party computation (SMPC) is another alternative, allowing multiple parties to jointly compute a function without revealing their individual inputs.

Applying data redaction techniques to federated learning models requires several vital considerations. Your redaction techniques must align with legal and industry-specific regulations like GDPR, HIPAA, or the California Consumer Privacy Act (CCPA). While protecting privacy is essential, overly aggressive redaction can compromise the utility of the data for machine learning tasks. Therefore, a balanced approach that maintains data is crucial. Keep an audit trail of what data has been redacted and how it is an important aspect, not only for compliance but also for troubleshooting and model interpretability.

22 Categorize Your Data Types

Data may be categorized into three main types based on their format and organization: structured, unstructured, and semi-structured.

Plan to categorize your data into three main types based on its format and organization: structured, unstructured, and semi-structured. Each of these data types brings unique challenges and opportunities to collect, store, and analyze for shaping how your business will leverage information to your AI/ML to make informed predictions.

Structured data is the most organized and straightforward type of data. It is highly formatted and follows a well-defined schema. Structured data elements are stored in rows and columns within a relational database or spreadsheet. The uniformity and consistency of structured data make it easy to query, process, and analyze using traditional Database Management Systems (DBMS) and Structured Query Language (SQL) queries. Examples of structured data include financial records, inventory databases, customer information, and transaction logs. In a contact center, structured data may include customer names, phone numbers, timestamps of interactions, and call duration. The predictability and efficiency of working with structured data make it ideal for reporting, generating business intelligence dashboards, and conducting statistical analyses.

In contrast to structured data, unstructured data lacks a predefined schema and does not fit neatly into rows and columns. This type of data is often free-form, comprised of text, images, audio, video, social media posts, emails, and other content that does not have a specific organizational structure. Examples of unstructured data may include customer feedback from social media comments, voice recordings of customer complaints, or email transcripts. Unstructured data presents significant challenges for data management and analysis. Its sheer volume and complexity require specialized tools and techniques for processing and extracting valuable insights. Planning for your AI system to understand customer sentiment, identify emerging issues, and effectively tailor services requires NLP algorithms, image recognition systems, and sentiment analysis tools to utilize unstructured data.

Semi-structured data represents a hybrid form that exhibits structured and unstructured data characteristics. It contains some level of organization, typically using tags or labels, but does not adhere to a rigid schema like fully structured data. Semi-structured data is commonly found in Extensible Markup Language (XML) and JavaScript Object Notation (JSON) formats. These formats provide some flexibility in data representation, making them useful for handling complex data that may evolve over time.

Semi-structured data can include call logs with varying data fields, such as call duration, customer ID, and agent notes. It allows contact centers to capture relevant interaction information without strictly adhering to a rigid structure. The challenge with semi-structured data lies in its processing. While it is more flexible than structured data, it still requires specialized techniques and tools to parse, store, and analyze effectively. Extracting meaningful information from semi-structured data often involves combining elements of both structured and unstructured data analysis.

Understanding the different types of data sources, including structured, unstructured, and semi-structured data, is critical for your business planning to harness the power of data-driven insights. Each type has its strengths and weaknesses, and leveraging the appropriate tools and techniques to handle these data types is essential for successful data management and analysis. By combining the strengths of all three types, organizations can unlock a wealth of valuable information and gain a competitive edge in today's data-driven landscape.

23 Federated Learning

Federated learning represents a paradigm shift in how machine learning models are trained and deployed in contact centers.

The term Federated Learning (FL) was coined by Google in 2016 in a paper, "Communication-Efficient Learning of Deep Networks from Decentralized Data." The paper describes how to train AI models without anyone seeing or touching your data. This learning paradigm allows ML models to tap raw data streamed from multiple decentralized nodes, such as different departments, geographic locations, individual databases, or even customer wearables, such as a heart monitor or smartwatch, without pooling all the data in a centralized server. Updates are decrypted, averaged, and integrated into the centralized single deep learning model. Iteration after iteration, the collaborative training continues until the model is fully trained.

Deep learning models need vast amounts of training data. However, companies in heavily regulated industries are hesitant to take the risk of using or sharing sensitive data to build an AI model for the promise of uncertain rewards. FL addresses these issues by allowing initial AI models to be trained centrally but fine-tuned locally at each node. Local data stays local, mitigating data privacy concerns. After local training, only the parameters or updates to the model are transmitted back to the central server, which then aggregates these updates to refine the "global" model, thereby minimizing data transfer overheads. As local models are updated in real-time with each customer interaction, the AI system can offer more accurate and timely responses or recommendations, increasing customer service effectiveness. Finally, since raw data doesn't leave its local environment, compliance with data protection laws becomes significantly easier.

This method starkly contrasts traditional centralized machine learning approaches, where all customer interactions and related data are sent to a central repository for training AI models. While effective in producing accurate models, this centralized approach has several drawbacks. Centralizing customer data raises privacy concerns with increasing regulations like GDPR and CCPA. Transmitting large datasets from geographically dispersed contact centers to a centralized server can be logistically challenging and resource-intensive. The lag in transmitting data and updating the centralized model can slow down real-time decision-making capabilities, which is crucial for customer service applications.

FL has its own set of challenges for contact centers that are not dissimilar to a centralized approach: Aggregating model updates from multiple nodes to a central server might also require substantial bandwidth, mainly when updates are frequent. There is a risk that the model could perform inconsistently across different nodes if they have very different local datasets. Transmitting model updates may expose sensitive data patterns or insights, requiring additional layers of encryption or security protocols. With localized training, ensuring that the quality of the model meets the desired standard across all nodes can be troublesome.

Still, FL represents a paradigm shift in how machine learning models are trained and deployed in contact centers. FL adeptly navigates the complexities posed by data privacy regulations and logistical constraints, offering a middle path that enjoys both the benefits of localized adaptability and global data insights. As such, it presents a compelling model for your AI-powered contact center, enabling your business to offer high-quality, responsive, and compliant customer interactions.

24 Do You Need Deep Learning?

Deep learning can solve complex problems, but it may not be the answer to every issue a contact center faces.

The advent of deep learning in AI and ML offers transformative potential for contact centers. Deep learning, a subfield of ML, deals with algorithms inspired by the structure and function of the brain, called artificial neural networks (ANN). Deep learning has demonstrated exceptional performance in various domains, from advanced NLP to real-time customer sentiment analysis. However, integrating deep learning requires a detailed, well-thought-out strategy and necessitates meticulous planning due to its inherent complexity and computational requirements.

Deep learning can solve complex problems, but it may not be the answer to every issue a contact center may face. Deep learning can provide significant value over traditional machine learning or rule-based systems. Using deep learning for tasks such as automatic summation in ACW or detecting nuanced customer emotions in voice recordings is an excellent application of the technology.

Plan to identify the specific business objectives that deep learning can address. Is your goal to reduce response times, improve customer satisfaction, or perhaps enhance human agent productivity through automation? Once the objectives are defined, establish your corresponding KPIs to measure success.

Deep learning models require significant computational power, especially when working with large datasets and complex architectures. Your business should plan for large-scale computing resources, including Graphics Processor Units (GPU), Tensor Processing Units (TPU), and large storage solutions. As an alternative, consider a cloud-based service that offers scalability and flexibility. Plan for a framework to ease model development but with the scalability and compatibility with other systems in your ecosystem.

Implementing deep learning algorithms demands a specialized skill set. Plan to train or hire data scientists, machine learning engineers, and domain experts familiar with contact center operations. Training a deep learning model involves several key steps. First, plan to collect and preprocess a large dataset representative of the problem you aim to solve. Next, choose the appropriate type, such as Convolutional Neural Network (CNN) or Recurrent Neural Network (RNN). Then, design the neural network's architecture by specifying layers and nodes.

Initialize the model's parameters and select an optimization algorithm, such as stochastic gradient descent. Train the model on the training set by iteratively adjusting the weights to minimize a loss function, which measures the difference between the model's predictions and actual outcomes. Evaluate the model's performance using the validation set, tuning hyperparameters as needed. Hyperparameters are the configuration settings used to structure machine learning models. Once satisfied, test the model on the test set to assess its generalization capabilities.

The model architecture will vary based on the specific tasks. RNN for sequential patterns is recommended for voice or text data. Once the models are built, they should be evaluated rigorously against the predefined KPIs to ensure they meet business objectives. After validation, the model needs to be deployed in the contact center's operational environment and integrated with your CRM software, data warehouses, and other existing systems. Plan to adhere to legal regulations such as data protection laws and ensure the ethical use of AI technologies is not compromised.

25 Integrating a Large Language Model

LLMs can improve your ROI and provide significant efficiency. However, these benefits must be balanced against associated risks and costs.

The relationship between deep learning and LLM, or Large Language Models, is symbiotic and foundational, with deep learning the underlying technology that makes LLM possible. The advancement of LLM capabilities has enabled new opportunities for contact center applications. Yet, implementing generative AI-powered enterprise-grade applications that access LLM capabilities may be difficult for many organizations.

Integrating LLMs can improve your ROI and provide significant efficiency and customer satisfaction benefits. However, these benefits must be balanced against associated risks and costs. As an illustration, inaccuracies or misunderstandings by chatbots can frustrate customers, posing a risk of churn. For planning, it's essential to carefully evaluate specific LLM solutions, their capabilities, data privacy implications, and the potential need for human oversight.

Utilizing LLM in your contact center can take several approaches, each offering distinct benefits, associated risks, and costs. One approach is employing LLMs for text generation and content creation to automate ACW summations to close out customer interactions. This approach reduces agent AHT and increases overall productivity. Planning should consider the risk of generated content and the need for careful curation and quality control. Initial setup and integration costs can be high, and over-reliance on LLMs for summarization may lead to missing or misinterpreting essential details. Planning should also be aware of privacy concerns, as Personal Identifiable Information (PII) might be included in summaries.

A second approach is deploying LLM-powered chatbots and Interactive Virtual Assistants (IVA) for 24/7 customer service and support. LLMs improve intent recognition in NLP and NLG. Additional capabilities such as content augmentation, tone of content, and content classification can be combined to implement IVAs capable of engaging in human-like conversational interactions. When planning, it's essential to have procedures that confirm the IVA's comprehension and response to customer inquiries. Inaccuracies or misunderstandings from IVAs can lead to customer frustration. Allocate a budget for LLM model development, integration with chatbot platforms, and ongoing training to improve performance against the potential savings from reduced agent workload.

Data analysis and insights represent another LLM application area. LLMs can parse vast amounts of textual data to extract valuable information, sentiments, and trends. While offering profound insights, plan to address the risk of misinterpretation or bias in the LLM's analysis with an investment in LLM models, data preprocessing, and analysis tools.

Finally, the capabilities of LLMs can be advantageous for language translation to support customers where English is not their first language. LLMs use language embeddings or encodings that help the model identify the language of the input text. These embeddings act as contextual cues, allowing the model to adjust its responses accordingly. For example, if it detects a query in French, it will generate responses in French.

Planning LLM deployment should document the benefits of improved efficiency and valuable data insights. LLMs facilitate multilingual communication and scalability without significant staffing increases. However, the risks encompass accuracy concerns, privacy and security issues, complex implementation, and ethical considerations tied to biases. Costs include LLM acquisition, integration, maintenance, and the necessity of ongoing human oversight. Careful planning, monitoring, and ethical considerations are essential to harness LLM-based applications effectively while mitigating associated risks.

26 Choose a Voice Persona

Choose a voice persona for your VUI that aligns with your brand identity and resonates with your target audience.

Planning a Voice User Interface (VUI) for conversational AI in your contact centers represents a pivotal shift in how businesses engage with customers. In a VUI integrated with an LLM, the Automated Speech Recognition (ASR) and text-to-speech (TTS) functionalities of the VUI work in tandem with the computational processing of the language model to deliver real-time, interactive dialogues. Both VUIs and language models generate data that can be analyzed for performance optimization. For example, your VUI can analyze frequent queries for better service provisioning or identify conversational bottlenecks.

VUI is a dynamic and multifaceted endeavor that blends technology and human interaction to create personalized and accessible customer service experiences. Your plan should begin with a clear understanding of your objectives. Identify what you propose to accomplish with your VUI. Is your intention to reduce call resolution times, enhance customer satisfaction, or provide self-service options? Each objective shapes the VUI's design and functionality. Identifying specific use cases, such as handling common inquiries or appointment scheduling, is equally critical. Be as concise as possible and present users with their options. Avoid open-ended questions. Suggest the kind of answer you're looking for. For example, what type of car are you looking to rent: compact, mid-size, or sedan? Limit the options, including a minimum of information in one question. Stay on topic without mixing options. Repeat the answer to your customer to be sure it is correct.

Using a VUI provides a straightforward approach to customer service because it uses speech, which is how we naturally communicate. Thus, your planning should define a well-designed, responsive, intuitive, and proactive VUI that engages customers in conversations and effectively replies to their queries. As simple as a voice chat may seem, creating conversational interfaces requires designers and developers to abandon current practices and embrace a new mindset. Design patterns commonly used in graphic user interfaces (GUI) are ineffective in conversation-driven interfaces.

Choose a voice persona for your VUI that aligns with your brand identity and resonates with your target audience. Whether it's a professional, friendly, or empathetic tone, consistency in voice is critical. Investing in NLP technology is fundamental to ensure the VUI comprehends and responds to a wide range of customer queries with human-like fluency.

Having your customers feel they are having a natural conversation with your AI-powered contact center is one of the central aspects of a VUI. It is not enough to make the conversation path functional; the conversation must also work from a social perspective. Isolated messages and repetitive responses don't seem human-like. In a real conversation, people transition from one topic to another, for example, using a polite greeting to ask about the weather and then moving to the next topic.

Plan to integrate your VUI with existing systems to be effective within your contact center. This includes CRM software, databases, and communication platforms. Integration ensures that the VUI accesses pertinent customer data and transitions systematically while enabling personalized responses.

27 Evaluate AI Vendor Technologies

Your AI vendor selection process should align with your business objectives, offer cutting-edge capabilities, provide robust support, and ensure a solid ROI.

As AI/ML becomes more prominent, so does the number of vendors offering those services. Planning to select the right vendor can be challenging, but investing the time and effort into the vendor selection process will ultimately lead to a successful AI/ML implementation that can meet your goals for innovation. Remember that choosing the right AI/ML vendor is a long-term commitment. Your strategy needs a vendor selection process that aligns with your business objectives, offers cutting-edge AI capabilities, provides robust support, and ensures a solid ROI.

Review each vendor's financial stability, reputation, and longevity in the market. Weigh their commitment to ongoing research and development. AI/ML technology will continue to evolve rapidly, and you will need a vendor with a clear roadmap and a vision for the future to ensure that their products align with your business's future needs.

Appraise each vendor's pricing model and contractual agreements. Appraise the transparency of their pricing structure, including licensing fees, implementation costs, and ongoing maintenance charges, to ensure it aligns with your budget and expected ROI.

Understanding each vendor's expertise and experience in AI/ML is paramount. Review each vendor's previous client references and case studies. Concentrate on vendors with a proven track record for successful AI/ML deliverables. AI is leveling the playing field for CCaaS vendors. New AI functionality reduces the advantages of long-term CCaaS vendors in favor of those with robust AI and ML solutions.

Evaluate each vendor's technical knowledge, qualifications, and certifications related to AI/ML technologies against a thorough document of your goals and objectives representative of use cases. Vendors with strong expertise and deep experience will be able to understand your specific requirements and propose high-quality solutions.

Effective collaboration and communication are always crucial for a successful vendor-client relationship. Gauge each vendor's responsiveness and willingness to participate in ongoing discussions. Weigh each vendor's capability to provide regular updates and progress reports. Clear and transparent communication will ensure your vendor is aligned with your goals throughout the project lifecycle.

Ensure the vendor's technology stack offers the flexibility and scalability to be compatible with your current infrastructure ecosystem. Vendors with an up-to-date technology stack are better equipped to handle complex AI/ML projects and adapt to future advancements. Consider the vendor's use of programming languages and development frameworks for data management and storage capabilities. AI and ML solutions rely on data handling and critical privacy considerations. Consider how each vendor collects, stores, and processes data, and verify they have robust data security measures to protect sensitive information.

Plan to assess each vendor's approach to model development. Determine if the vendor uses pre-built models or can customize an LLM to meet your business needs. Review each vendor's ability to optimize and fine-tune your potential ML model and integrate domain knowledge specific to your business. Establish if each vendor can customize your model for optimal performance and accuracy. Vendors who have the flexibility to customize their models to meet your needs are better equipped to meet your business requirements.

28 Set Expectations for a Proof of Concept

Your PoC should evaluate the technology's applicability, functionality, and ROI measured by specific KPIs.

Setting expectations for a PoC or a full implementation is integral to implementing your AI-powered contact center. It necessitates strategic guidance from your executive management. It is not just a technical exercise but also a strategic initiative. A PoC is the preliminary stage to evaluate the technology's applicability, functionality, and ROI measured by specific KPIs. Establishing appropriate expectations is essential for steering the project toward a meaningful conclusion.

The first step is ensuring the plan aligns with your broader business strategy. Your plan should clarify how the AI implementation fits within the organizational roadmap and contributes to cost efficiency, customer satisfaction, or market differentiation objectives.

Plan to define the key milestones that mark the progress of the initiative. These milestones could range from preliminary data collection and model training to initial deployment and performance assessment. Each milestone should have responsible parties and deadlines attached, providing a structured timeline to guide the project team. Identify and engage key stakeholders from the outset to provide real-world insights into operational requirements and potential pitfalls. This includes management and technical teams and your customer service representatives, whom the implementation will directly impact.

Start by defining the objectives and scope of the initiative and what you aim to achieve, whether it's automating specific customer service tasks, improving customer satisfaction, or reducing operational costs. Also, specify what is 'out-of-scope' to avoid feature creep and over-complication. Determine how the success of the AI initiative will be measured. This could be reduced handling time for customer queries, increased first-call resolution rates, or improved customer satisfaction scores. These metrics will set the benchmark for what is considered a successful implementation.

Set your expectations about the PoC's budget, including upfront costs related to migration, building a data model, personnel, and any other miscellaneous expenditures. A well-defined budget enables better financial oversight and sets clear limitations on what can be achieved within the scope of the PoC.

Data readiness is another critical factor. Verify if the existing data is adequate and high-quality to train the AI model. Set expectations around the volume, variety, and velocity of data that will be needed. In some cases, additional data collection or data cleaning may be required.

Prepare a risk assessment outlining potential hurdles and their impact. This could include technical risks like data security, operational risks like employee resistance, and business risks like compliance or security damage. Plan a mitigation strategy for each risk to address concerns preemptively.

Assuming the PoC is successful, plan a clearly articulated scaling strategy. This could involve gradually increasing the range of tasks the AI system handles or expanding its usage across multiple departments or geographic locations. A well-defined scaling strategy allows a smoother transition from the PoC to full-scale implementation. Lastly, every phase of the PoC should be meticulously documented for accountability and to ensure that the lessons learned can be referenced to secure further stakeholder buy-in for scaling the initiative.

29 Develop the Criteria for a Proof of Concept

Develop your PoC criteria with a comprehensive cost-benefit analysis that considers the initial investment and ongoing maintenance, training, and potential savings or revenue increases.

Integrating AI into your contact center may be compelling. However, innovation is more complicated than it looks. Before spending your time and budget building a total AI solution, plan to minimize your business risks by developing a PoC. A proof-of-concept tests innovative ideas on a small scale before committing to a full-scale project.

Create your criteria from customer experiences. These experiences do not need to include everything a customer will ever do, but they should cover the essential requirements. Involve both IT and business decision-makers in this process so that you can prioritize functionalities based on the customer experiences you want to create. During this stage, hone your success criteria to make them specific, actionable, and measurable. Are you looking to improve response times, enhance agent productivity, or provide personalized customer experiences? An AI PoC should be a prototype or a demonstration of your proposed AI solution designed to test whether your approach is feasible and likely to be successful. Its purpose is to validate the concept, assess the proposed ecosystem's potential benefits, and identify potential challenges or limitations in your existing environment.

Plan a complete cross-section of capabilities for your PoC. Selecting a use case that doesn't add much value or doesn't use the full potential of AI is not a good plan. Moreover, a poorly executed AI PoC can kill your innovation project before it starts. AI is expensive, and choosing an insignificant case may not validate your approach or technologies.

Plan to establish clear performance metrics and benchmarks to evaluate the effectiveness of the AI PoC. Metrics should be tied directly to your objectives. For instance, if reducing customer wait times is a goal, measure the average wait time before and after AI implementation. These metrics will serve as quantifiable evidence of the AI's impact.

To fully determine the feasibility of your AI PoC implementation, plan to assess the availability and quality of your data. Ensure the AI PoC data is structured, comprehensive, and readily integrates with your ML data models. Allocate the time to perform data cleansing and preprocessing to eliminate inconsistencies that will impact the success of your PoC.

While AI implementation can potentially yield significant benefits, weighing the benefits against the costs involved is essential. Develop a comprehensive cost-benefit analysis from your AI PoC that considers the initial investment and ongoing maintenance, training, and potential savings or revenue increases. This analysis will help make informed decisions about the long-term viability of the AI solution.

Plan for your PoC to adhere to your organization's ethical guidelines and regulatory compliance. Ensure the AI PoC respects customer privacy and complies with data protection laws. A breach of ethics or compliance can have severe repercussions for your business.

The AI landscape is constantly evolving. Your criteria should include flexibility and adaptability. Is the AI PoC capable of learning and evolving with changing customer behaviors and industry trends? Can it be easily upgraded or customized to meet new requirements?

30 Plan PoC Use Cases

Simply adopting an AI-driven solution and expecting an immediate ROI is not enough. You need to know how to apply AI to target your contact center's pain points.

The migration from a traditional PBX system to an AI-driven model is a significant strategic decision. The change promises a plethora of benefits, such as increased efficiency, cost-effectiveness, and enhanced customer experiences. However, simply adopting an AI-driven solution and expecting immediate ROI is not enough. You need to know how to apply AI to target your contact center's pain points. The following provides a few examples of use cases.

Plan one use case for intelligent call routing. Deploy AI algorithms to assess incoming calls based on several factors, such as caller history, intent, and current queue lengths, to route the call to the most suitable agent. Assess the success of the call routing to your ACD, employing hierarchical prompts to determine the caller's intent and routing the calls to a queued skill. Compare the AI routing to your PBX call flows to assess the success in the use case.

Another use case is integrating AI-driven chatbots or voice assistants to handle routine inquiries. Gauge the containment rate for the chatbot or voice assistant for customers who did not have to engage a human agent and FCR rates compared to a PBX-only approach. Implement AI tools that analyze customer data in real-time to provide a personalized service experience, such as recommending products or recalling past interactions. Compare customer satisfaction and engagement metrics before and after the migration.

How you talk to customers significantly impacts your brand. Nothing delivers customer satisfaction like consistent positive communication. Manually performing quality management of every call is not possible in most organizations. Consider a use case to utilize ML algorithms and NLP to analyze call recordings, agent performance, and customer feedback. There are several parts to this use case, with the ultimate objective of extracting insights from your call recordings. One sub-use case tests AI algorithms for real-time voice analytics to evaluate the customer and agent's mood, pace, and sentiment during calls. Another sub-case uses AI algorithms to identify specific keywords or phrases in call recordings, enabling quick identification of critical information, compliance breaches, or customer trends. Plan to use AI to assist in monitoring calls for compliance with regulatory requirements and internal policies, ensuring that agents adhere to scripts and guidelines.

Assigning the right people with the right skills is critical for your PoC's success and your business's overall profitability. Plan a use case for ML algorithms to predict optimal staffing levels based on historical data, thus aiding in effective resource allocation. Measure the efficiency gains against those offered by PBX-based systems, which often lack predictive capabilities.

Reaching your customers at the right time in an outbound campaign can be the difference between a successful campaign and one that fails. Calling your customers at an inconvenient time can turn a well-qualified prospect off of your message entirely. Plan a use case for AI to analyze the best times to call customers and improve the success rate of outbound campaigns. Gauge the answer rate against your existing dialer.

31 Prepare for Challenges

Prepare for challenges with your PoC when high business expectations are weighed against poor customer experiences.

Before deploying your PoC or a full implementation, prepare for potential challenges that may emerge and require immediate attention to ensure your AI solution is accepted and aligned with your business objectives and technical goals. Chatbots and voice bots promise operational efficiency and improved customer experiences, but their implementation comes with complexities.

There are many reasons why bots may fail to meet your expectations. While business expectations are high, your customers may face disappointing interactions in a PoC and, worse, in your full deployment. One reason stems from using decision-tree programming.

Human conversation organized in a decision tree structure feels unnatural. Humans form sentences, choosing words subconsciously. Your customers may ask questions in multiple ways or use different terminology or jargon. Using a systematic "if-then-else" approach to anticipate all the ways your customer can form a query is almost impossible, resulting in your bot misrecognizing words in your NLP. Given the millions of outcomes that a conversation can have, your bots may fail to meet your customer experience and your business objectives.

One challenge for deploying voice bots and chatbots is customer authentication and verification before they access their accounts or receive assistance. Introducing new methods, such as voice biometrics, may confuse your customers. Be prepared to maintain existing verification procedures while you introduce more contemporary technologies.

Another challenge is implementing personalized services and customer concerns over data privacy. Consumers are increasingly concerned about how their data is used and stored. Ethical considerations exist when personalizing experiences to the point where they might be perceived as intrusive or manipulative. For example, excessive personalization may make customers feel that their privacy has been violated, which can result in reputational damage to your business. AI personalization's efficacy also depends on how quickly and willingly users adapt to interacting with voice bots and chatbots. While younger generations might be more tech-savvy, older demographics might find these technologies overwhelming and fail to benefit from personalization features effectively.

Prepare for very involved queries that will need creative and innovative problem-solving. Voice bots and chatbots may lack creativity and cannot generate unique solutions or think outside the predefined boundaries of their programming. As a result, bots may offer generic or repetitive suggestions that do not adequately address the complication of the problem. In addition, some issues are inherently complex, requiring specialized knowledge. Some customers may prefer talking to a human agent for particular queries or concerns. When your bot cannot handle a customer's inquiry or complaint, your bot should be able to seamlessly escalate the issue to a human agent who can provide personalized and empathetic responses using the context of the conversation.

Finally, integrating voice bots and chatbots with existing systems can be challenging, requiring coordination between different teams and systems. Bots need to be able to access customer data and interact with other systems, such as CRM and ticketing systems. To prepare for this challenge, have a clear plan for integrating bots with existing systems and ensure that all teams work together effectively.

32 Structure an Approach for Data Readiness

All datasets are flawed, so data readiness is essential for machine learning. Your ML will be nearly useless if you can't make sense of your data records.

Whether you are preparing a subset of data for a PoC or a complete implementation, the ML in your AI-powered contact center will rely heavily on data. Data is what makes algorithm training possible and why ML has become newsworthy in recent years. Regardless of the size of your ML dataset or the expertise of your data scientist, your ML will be nearly useless if you can't make sense of your data records.

All datasets are flawed, so data readiness is essential in making it suitable for machine learning. This includes procedures for proper data collection mechanisms, which may consume most of the time spent on machine learning, sometimes requiring months before the first algorithm is built.

Preparing the readiness of your data for ML is an essential procedure involving several sub-processes to transform raw data into a format that ML algorithms can easily consume to create accurate models. Before delving into the technical aspects of machine learning, it is essential to understand your business context, objectives, and the questions you seek to answer, particularly in the complex ecosystem of contact centers. Objectives could range from improving customer satisfaction by automating routine tasks to identifying patterns in customer queries.

Stage 1 aligns these objectives by collaborating with key stakeholders, including customer service management, data analysts, and business leaders. This perspective will guide your data preparation efforts, prioritize relevant attributes, and focus on appropriate statistical methods.

Stage 2 of data readiness is data collection, emphasizing avoiding the old computer adage "garbage in, garbage out." Contact centers often deal with a voluminous amount of heterogeneous data generated from multiple interaction channels, such as voice calls, emails, and chats. From these channels, identify your data from various sources like CRM systems, call logs, email archives, chat transcripts, voice recordings, and social media engagements, and ensure the compatibility of different data formats. Your focus is to gather comprehensive, accurate, and relevant data that aligns with your project objectives.

Stage 3 is performing an initial data assessment that starts with data exploration and involves getting a 'feel' for the data. In your assessment, look for patterns in call durations, customer feedback, and types of queries. Statistical summaries, visualizations, and basic descriptive analytics can provide insights into your data quality and initial patterns or trends. Isolate any inconsistencies. Your data may contain various problems, including missing values, duplicate records, and outliers that might affect the quality of your machine-learning model. These need to be identified and cleaned before proceeding further.

Stage 4 is cleaning your data. Plan a strategy to handle missing entries, such as imputing average values for missing numerical data or using techniques like string matching for categorical data. Identify and remove duplicate entries that can bias the model. Remove incomplete records based on the nature and severity of the missing data. Remediate outliners and noise that can skew the data distribution, making it challenging for machine learning models to identify patterns using transformations like normalization and scaling.

33 Integrate, Engineer, and Format Your Data

Planning needs to be interdisciplinary, coordinating the readiness effort with your data scientists, domain experts, and stakeholders to integrate, engineer, and format your data.

Data readiness for ML in contact centers continues the process from the previous rule with the added requirement of a deep understanding of the operation's technological and business dimensions. Your planning needs to be interdisciplinary, coordinating the readiness effort with your data scientists, domain experts, and stakeholders to integrate, engineer, and format your data to meet the requirements of your ML algorithms.

Stage 5 involves data integration and aggregation, particularly in cases where data is collected from multiple sources for integration into a single dataset. Data traffic depends on various platforms, and managing the huge amount of traffic and structuring the data into a meaningful format will be critical. Data points need to be merged, joined, or concatenated based on a common attribute. For instance, you may need to merge different data sources based on shared identifiers such as customer ID or account ID. You may also need to compile features that require aggregation. For example, you could calculate the average call duration per customer as a new feature. Also, consider synthetic data to test new products and tools, validate models, satisfy AI needs, and simulate not yet encountered conditions.

Stage 6 engineers the most relevant features contributing to the model's predictive power. Plan to choose relevant features that directly impact your objectives. For instance, if the aim is to predict call volume, variables like time and day of the week could be crucial. Plan to remove redundant or irrelevant features and derive new features from existing ones to provide additional information that can help enhance the model's performance. For example, new features can be extracted from text data using NLP techniques like sentiment analysis or keyword extraction.

For Stage 7, plan to divide your dataset into at least two subsets: training and testing. Optionally, a third set called the validation set can be created.

Plan to format your data in Stage 8 as per the requirements of your ML algorithm. This could involve converting text data into numerical tokens, one-hot encoding for categorical variables, or reshaping data structures. One-hot encoding is a foundational technique for transforming categorical data into a machine-readable format. However, like any other technique, it comes with its own set of challenges and considerations. Carefully plan the application of encoding, considering the domain-specific needs and limitations, yielding effective ML models that meet or exceed your operational requirements. As an illustration, categorical variables like Call_Type or Agent_Skillset can be one-hot encoded for machine learning tasks such as call routing optimization or customer satisfaction prediction.

Finally, plan to maintain the quality of your data. Statistical properties can change over time due to data drift and anomalies. Your plan should include continuously monitoring for data drift to confirm that your model is still suitable and accurate. Track metrics such as missing value rates, outlier frequencies, and other quality indicators, and implement real-time anomaly detection algorithms to detect unusual data points or patterns that may indicate errors, anomalies, or fraudulent activity.

34

Maintain Post-Preparation Data Quality

Plan to monitor your data continuously for data drift and anomaly detection.

Once your ML data has been prepared, cleansed, and engineered, maintaining the data's quality is paramount. Any degradation in data quality can lead to inferior model performance, flawed insights, and erroneous decision-making. Plan your key strategies and best practices for ensuring data quality is maintained post-preparation. Effective monitoring of metrics like missing value rates, outlier frequencies, and timely remediation can go a long way in sustaining the performance and reliability of ML models in such settings.

Plan to monitor your data continuously for data drift and anomaly detection. Data drift is an unavoidable challenge in machine learning applications that require sustained attention, especially in environments like contact centers, which are dynamic and subject to rapid changes in customer behavior. Concept drift occurs when the relationship between the input and output variables changes over time. For example, customer preferences for certain services may evolve, affecting service predictions' quality. Covariate drift happens when the distribution of the input variables changes, but the relationship between the input and output remains constant. Consider that if a contact center expands its service to new geographical areas, the demographic distribution of calls could change. Prior probability shift is a case of covariate drift where only the class distribution changes, not the feature distribution or the decision boundary. For instance, a seasonal shift in the types of queries a contact center receives would be an example of a prior probability shift.

Plan for techniques like clustering, neural networks, or statistical tests for anomaly detection to identify data points, events, or observations that deviate significantly from the general distribution of a dataset. Anomaly detection can be instrumental in flagging unusual customer interactions or system behaviors that may indicate fraud, data errors, or service quality issues.

Track data versioning of changes in your dataset to enable data rollback to a previous state in case of contamination. Plan to limit data access to authorized personnel to prevent unauthorized manipulation. Maintain logs that record who accessed or modified the data, timestamp, and description of the changes. Plan for compliance checks by regularly reviewing data handling and storage practices to ensure they comply with data protection regulations such as GDPR or HIPAA.

Maintain automatic validation rules for range checks that flag data points falling outside an acceptable range for numerical variables. Implement consistency checks that validate relationships between variables remain logical and consistent. For instance, it would be illogical for a 'call duration' to be a negative number.

Develop feedback loops to model predictions. Monitor the performance of deployed models closely and use this feedback to double-check if any degradation in performance might be due to data quality issues. Periodically sample random subsets of data for manual review to validate accuracy and completeness. Involve domain experts in these audits to ensure that the data still aligns with real-world contexts and scenarios. Only through such sustained efforts can the integrity of machine learning models and their insights be reliably upheld.

35 Gauge the Success of Your PoC

Gauging the success of your PoC requires examining the impact on various metrics and aspects of contact center operations.

Assessing the operational impact after deploying your PoC AI solution requires a comprehensive approach that examines the impact on various metrics and aspects of contact center operations. By carefully evaluating the following factors, your business can determine whether or not your PoC delivers improved efficiency and customer experiences.

• Evaluate the financial impact of the AI solution by tracking cost savings and return on investment (ROI). Compare the costs of implementing and maintaining the AI system with its benefits. Successful PoC AI solutions should show a positive ROI, which might include savings in labor costs or reduced infrastructure expenses.

• Compare AHT for agent assist. A reduction in AHT suggests improved efficiency as AI may assist agents in resolving issues faster.

• Assess FCR to measure the percentage of customer issues resolved during the first interaction without requiring follow-up calls. A successful AI implementation should increase FCR, as the AI system helps agents provide accurate solutions promptly.

• Assess the impact of AI on queue times. AI-driven solutions can help distribute calls more efficiently, reducing customers' time waiting to speak with an agent. Shorter queue times improve the overall customer experience and operational efficiency.

- Evaluate how AI affects agent workload. Are agents handling more interactions with the assistance of AI? Is there a noticeable decrease in agent stress levels? Monitoring agent workload post-deployment helps ensure that the AI system effectively supports agents without overwhelming them.

- Track the number of incoming calls or inquiries post-AI implementation. An increase in call volume could indicate that customers are engaging more with the contact center due to improved service or new features offered by AI. Assess whether the contact center's capacity aligns with this change in demand.

- Examine error rates in post-deployment operations. This includes errors in customer interactions, data entry, or information retrieval. AI should contribute to a reduction in these errors, which, in turn, enhances operational efficiency and customer satisfaction.

- Assess agent productivity metrics like the number of resolved cases per hour or the average time spent on after-call work (ACW). A successful AI implementation should improve agent productivity as they can focus on more complex tasks while AI handles routine inquiries.

- Evaluate the impact of AI on agent training and onboarding. Has it shortened the learning curve for new agents? Are agents becoming proficient in using AI tools quickly? Reduced training times and faster onboarding indicate improved operational efficiency.

- Solicit customer feedback regarding their experience with the contact center after AI implementation. Their input can provide valuable insights into the effectiveness of the AI system in enhancing operational efficiency. High customer satisfaction often correlates with improved efficiency.

- Analyze whether the AI system helps meet or exceed service level agreements (SLAs). AI can contribute to better SLA adherence by routing calls appropriately, reducing wait times, and improving issue resolution times.

- Consider how the AI solution scales with increased demand. Assess whether it maintains its efficiency as the contact center grows. Scalability is vital for long-term operational efficiency.

36 Refine Your PoC for Process Improvement

Plan to tune AI algorithms to optimize performance according to use-case requirements and desired outcomes.

Before full-scale deployment, plan to validate the effectiveness of your PoC. The first step is revisiting its objectives. Ensure that the PoC aligns with the broader goals of the contact center. Did the PoC reduce operational costs, enhance customer satisfaction, or increase agent productivity? If the initial PoC didn't yield the expected results, plan to systematically reassess your criteria, data, feature engineering, and algorithms to fine-tune your AI solution.

Tuning AI algorithms is crucial for a successful PoC. Plan to optimize performance according to use-case requirements and desired outcomes. Begin by conducting a comprehensive review of the initial algorithm's performance. Examine KPIs like accuracy, precision, recall, and F1 score. F1 score is a machine learning evaluation metric that measures a model's accuracy. It combines the precision and recall scores of a model. The accuracy metric computes how often a model correctly predicts a response from your dataset. These metrics will provide a baseline against which you can measure the impact of tuning.

Your quality of training data will significantly impact your AI algorithms' performance. Plan to conduct a thorough data analysis to identify any discrepancies, outliers, or inconsistencies that may have skewed the initial results. Refine your data cleaning and preprocessing steps to create a more reliable dataset for training and validation. Plan to optimize feature engineering, which involves crafting new features from existing data to improve the algorithm's predictive power. For example, adding features like 'average call duration' or 'frequency of interactions' could be beneficial if your AI solution is meant to predict customer behavior.

Employ techniques like K-fold cross-validation for more robust results. Cross-validation is primarily used in applied machine learning to estimate the skill of a machine learning model on unseen data. That is, to use a limited sample to assess how the model is expected to perform in general when used to make predictions on data not used during the model's training. K-fold cross-validation is particularly valuable when the available dataset is limited in size or when it's crucial to ensure that the model's performance is robust across different subsets of the data.

Techniques such as hyperparameter tuning can also optimize your configuration settings used to structure machine learning models. Numerous hyperparameter tuning algorithms exist, although the most commonly used types are Bayesian optimization, grid search, and randomized search. Hyperparameter tuning is iterative, trying out different combinations of parameters and values. Plan to start by defining a target variable, such as accuracy, as your primary metric, with your intent to maximize or minimize the variable. Once your optimal hyperparameters are identified, run the algorithm on your test set to evaluate its performance rigorously.

After each round of tuning, evaluate the algorithm's performance using the validation set. Examine the KPIs and compare them against the pre-assessment metrics. Iterate this process until satisfactory performance levels are reached.

37

Plan a Human-AI Mechanism

A principal challenge in the human-AI mechanism is ensuring the AI system is able to recognize when it has reached the limits of its capabilities.

Any plan to interact with customer inquiries and complaints with AI-powered chatbots and virtual assistants should include a mechanism to coordinate a human-AI procedure and develop escalation to agents. One of the principal challenges in coordinating the human-AI mechanism is ensuring that the AI system is able to recognize when it has reached the limits of its capabilities. For example, some issues are inherently complex and require specialized expertise for resolution, some customers may prefer talking to a human agent in certain types of queries or concerns, and customer frustration or urgency based on tone and language triggers escalation.

When the AI system is unable to handle a customer's inquiry or complaint, it should be able to escalate the issue to a human agent. Plan to design your AI systems with a blend of technological and human-centered strategies to escalate to your human agents seamlessly. Escalation should start with defining clear 'triggers' or 'thresholds,' which, when met, automatically initiate the handoff from AI to human agents. Triggers can be based on various factors, such as a customer query's complexity or preference. Triggers may also originate by analyzing the customer's tone of voice, choice of words, or patterns that indicate frustration or dissatisfaction.

Plan to identify issues likely to require human intervention by analyzing customer data to identify patterns and trends. If an issue is consistently triggered, it may indicate that your AI system needs to be improved to handle it more effectively.

Once the decision for escalation has been made, the AI system should transfer the customer and the context of the conversation to your human agent, who can provide personalized and empathetic responses. This context may include chat history, customer profiles, and other pertinent information. To ensure that escalation to agents is effective, it is important to have a well-defined escalation process in place. This process should include clear guidelines on when and how to escalate issues to human agents and the criteria for determining which agent should handle the issue. This data enables the human agent to provide more personalized service and shortens the resolution time, thus improving the overall customer experience.

Plan to effectively design this handoff with specific AI and human agent training. While AI requires continuous tuning to improve its escalation criteria and customer understanding, human agents need to be trained to deal with queries escalated from AI, making full use of the transferred context.

Human-AI coordination should be viewed as a dynamic, evolving mechanism that learns from its mistakes and successes. It is a multifaceted undertaking requiring strategic alignment, technical infrastructure, and continuous optimization. Plan for a feedback loop to be established where the efficacy of the escalation process is regularly reviewed. Both qualitative feedback from agents and customers and quantitative metrics like FCR, AHT, and CSAT scores should be considered for iterative improvement.

Plan for Security

The integration of AI bots in contact centers, while revolutionary, introduces a range of security considerations that need urgent and ongoing attention.

The deployment of AI in contact centers, particularly chatbots and voice bots, brings a host of security implications that are critically important to acknowledge and address. While these technologies offer transformative potential for automating and optimizing customer service, they also introduce new vulnerabilities and risks. Planning to understand and mitigate security implications is paramount for ensuring data integrity, confidentiality, and availability.

Contact centers frequently handle sensitive customer data, including personal information, payment details, and transaction history. As such, data storage accessed by your AI bots becomes a significant concern. Plan for your data to be encrypted and stored in secure databases with controlled access. Moreover, data transmission between the bot and the underlying servers must be secured to prevent interception, ideally through robust end-to-end encryption.

AI bots often have access to various internal databases to provide customer service effectively. This raises the risk of unauthorized access if the bot itself becomes compromised. Plan for strict access control mechanisms, like role-based access control (RBAC) or attribute-based access control (ABAC), to limit the bot's access to only the data essential for its function.

Plan for your security team to prepare for a data poisoning attack, where an attacker corrupts or feeds malicious data into your bot's learning algorithms to compromise your model's performance or commit specific errors. This type of attack can be particularly debilitating for bots that adapt and learn from real-time interactions with customers. Planning for regular audits of the learning data and using anomaly detection algorithms can help mitigate this risk.

Consider the threats from impersonation and social engineering. AI bots, especially those utilizing NLP, can be susceptible to sophisticated impersonation attempts. Attackers may engage the bot using specific language or questions designed to extract sensitive information. Plan for mechanisms for detecting unusual patterns of interaction or queries that might indicate a social engineering attempt.

Voice bots are particularly vulnerable to eavesdropping from hackers and malicious actors, especially if deployed using weak encryption protocols. These attackers can harness the power of AI to develop advanced cyberattacks, bypass your security measures, and exploit vulnerabilities that capture audio from sensitive conversations with your customers, which may later be processed and analyzed for exploitable information. Attackers may also use psychoacoustics to manipulate the audio signals that are perceptually indistinguishable from humans to take advantage of the ASR system's reliance on certain acoustic features, such as phonetic characteristics, temporal patterns, or spectral properties to exploit potential weaknesses in the system's decision-making process.

AI bots also rely on third-party applications, which can present potential security risks if the external services are insecure. Plan to perform due diligence in selecting third-party services and regular security assessments to help alleviate these risks.

Customer endpoints, like smartphones and computers interacting with the bot, are another area of concern. If a customer's device is compromised, it could be used to send malicious instructions to the bot. While your business has limited control over endpoint security, plan to implement additional layers of authentication and encryption to reduce risks.

39 Address Conversational AI Ethics

A single word may have different meanings depending on context and time. What is acceptable in one context might be perceived as unacceptable or deviant in another.

Understand the full impact of conversational AI on your customers and address the ethical challenges in your solution from the start. Language is inherently social, cultural, contextual, and historical, meaning your AI dialogue design will reflect your business image. Language is situational and contextual. Depending on context and time, a single word or conversation may have different meanings. What is acceptable in one context might be perceived as unacceptable or deviant in another. Plan for your developers to design your AI using ethical standards and a deep understanding of customer characteristics, contexts, and interests.

Voice bots and chatbots will interact with your customers to collect data, ranging from personal identifiers to sensitive information such as credit card details. Plan to obtain explicit consent from the customer before any data collection begins. The process for consent should be transparent, informing customers of the kind of data being collected and the purposes for which it will be used. In addition, your bots may have access to data that your human agent wouldn't usually have. For example, your business may have information from your CRM system, including your customer's transaction history. Your bots might add other customer insights from unconventional places on the internet. Plan to find the right balance between having too much and not enough customer data. Your customers may value personalized offers and experiences, which are at risk if your business doesn't have enough information. On the other hand, if your business uses too much information, your customers may feel uncomfortable.

Plan to address conversational transparency of your AI to reduce your customer's concerns, including privacy and personal data protection. Customers get concerned about their data being collected, stored, shared, or sold without consent. Plan to be open and transparent about data usage, ownership, and protection, and publish your policy on customer data.

Consider the impact of your chatbot persona. Alexander Graham Bell at the Boston Telephone Dispatch Company hired the first female telephone operator, Emma Nutt, on September 1, 1878, for lower costs and higher customer satisfaction. Bell determined women were better behaved than young men. Women had pleasant voices that customers—primarily men—preferred. They could also be paid less and supervised more strictly than their male counterparts. So, it is not unrelated that chatbots have disproportionately been given female names or voices, such as Apple's Siri and Amazon's Alexa, which can reinforce gender roles. Plan to avoid any gender bias during your bot's design.

Chatbots and voice bots lack the emotional intelligence to handle sensitive or critical issues that a human agent might navigate adeptly, with their limitations becoming evident in complex emotional interactions. Plan to delineate clear boundaries for AI-based interactions and provide an easy transition to human agents for situations beyond the scope of automated responses.

Ultimately, ethics comes down to the biases, prejudices, and morals originating from your designer's understanding of morality and fairness. Be cognitive of the social, cultural, and contextual implications your bots will have on your business image, and engage experts to design your AI framework from the beginning.

40 Scale Your Solution

Calculate the financial implications of scaling your AI solution, considering the costs of technology, training, and maintenance.

Scaling your AI solution from a PoC to a full-scale implementation is multifaceted. Planning for the complexities associated with this transition is both technical and organizational. Your plan can be conceptualized as a series of sequential steps requiring thorough attention to detail and effective collaboration among cross-functional teams. Before embarking on the scaling process, it is important to understand KPIs and the ROI metrics identified during the PoC stage. Conducting a cost-benefit analysis is an often overlooked aspect of scaling your solution. Plan to calculate the financial implications of deploying the AI solution at scale, considering the costs of technology, training, and maintenance. Compare these with the benefits—both quantitative, such as your projected reduced average handling time, and qualitative, like improved customer satisfaction—to arrive at a nuanced understanding of the potential ROI of a full deployment.

Your second task is to plan for stakeholder alignment, including technical leads, business analysts, and executive management. Be sure to prepare for the human and technical resources required in a full-scale implementation. Next, ensure your architecture will support the scaling for migration and production. Validate that your AI system complies with data protection laws and security standards. Plan for more than just technical feasibility when moving your PoC to production, including model risks, data bias, privacy, and ethics.

Planning for training agents and operational staff is paramount to ensure the seamless integration of the technology into existing workflows. The objective is to empower your human workforce to collaborate effectively with the AI system. Training programs should be comprehensive, covering the functional aspects of the AI tool, its capabilities, and limitations. Interactive simulations and real-world scenarios are valuable for ingraining best practices. Additionally, agents must be educated on handling situations where human intervention becomes essential. Plan for ongoing training and periodic refreshers as your AI systems continually evolve, requiring staff to adapt to new features and functionalities.

Consider a phased deployment of your rollout. Identify critical functional areas that can be deployed in isolation. Plan a pilot implementation in a controlled environment or a specific contact center segment. Allocate the resources and time to undertake rigorous quality assurance testing to ensure the AI system is stable and performing as expected. Involve agents to validate that the system is meeting its intended objectives.

Finalize your rollout to the entire contact center, continuously monitoring performance metrics, including accuracy, speed, and user satisfaction, which should be constantly evaluated against predetermined benchmarks, and making the necessary adjustments. Plan for regularly retraining your AI model with updated data sets to ensure your AI system adapts to evolving customer behavior and preferences. Plan to perform software patches and security updates to maintain system integrity. Keep the channel open for feedback from both agents and customers to provide qualitative insights to supplement quantitative data.

Scaling an AI solution in a contact center is an evolutionary process that does not end with full-scale implementation. As AI technology and customer preferences evolve, adjustments and upgrades are necessary to ensure the system consistently meets organizational objectives and customer satisfaction metrics.

41 Plan Ongoing Governance and Oversight

Deploying an AI framework is not a one-time endeavor but a continuous process requiring meticulous oversight.

AI in your contact centers can potentially transform customer service, operational efficiency, and data analytics. Consider that deploying an AI framework is not a one-time endeavor but a continuous process requiring meticulous oversight. Your plan should include ongoing governance and oversight, including monitoring, continuous improvement, staff training, and AI training that emerge as the four pillars of effective management for an AI-powered contact center.

Plan for real-time and periodic monitoring as an essential component for evaluating the performance metrics of AI-enabled systems. Weigh your existing major cost drivers, including call volume, labor costs, technology and infrastructure costs, training and development costs, and facilities costs, against the costs for your AI-powered solution for insights into your system efficacy. Monitoring KPIs like AHT, FCR, and CSAT will allow your business to pinpoint inefficiencies and make data-driven adjustments. In addition, security and compliance measures need constant vigilance to ensure the integrity and confidentiality of customer data. Plan to evaluate and deploy monitoring tools specifically for AI systems. Such systems should offer dashboards for real-time analytics and reports focusing on department-specific needs. Alerts for unusual patterns or performance degradation should also be available to ensure immediate attention and rapid remediation. Without ongoing monitoring, AI systems risk becoming obsolete or, worse, counterproductive.

AI systems are not static; they are designed to evolve and require continuous improvement. Your business should allocate resources to improve your AI-powered contact center constantly. Machine learning models should be fine-tuned based on the data collected and insights generated to improve their predictive accuracy and decision-making capabilities. Whether it is chatbots, automated routing algorithms, or sentiment analysis tools, an iterative approach to improvement is essential.

Plan for staff training to be an ongoing process. Despite the automation of various functions, human agents are irreplaceable for handling complex and sensitive issues. Hence, staff need to be trained to work in tandem with AI tools. This involves understanding how to interpret AI-generated analytics, manage handoffs between humans and AI agents, and operate new software interfaces. Customized training modules should be developed, focusing on the specific AI technologies deployed. Moreover, training should be ongoing, capturing the evolving functionalities of AI tools and the emerging best practices in customer service. Empowering the human staff through constant training ensures that the synergy between man and machine is optimized.

Just as human staff require ongoing training, so do AI systems. Your AI/ML system will only be as effective as the data training it. As you begin, training your AI system on all probable scenarios and data is impossible—plan to continuously capture changing customer behaviors, market conditions, and compliance requirements in your training data. Biases in AI models can also severely impair customer relations and even lead to legal repercussions. Hence, constant vigilance is required to scrutinize training data for potential biases and anomalies.

Finally, AI algorithms are susceptible to 'model drift,' where the model's performance can degrade over time due to changes in the data distribution. Regular retraining of the model is essential to maintain its performance and reliability.

Continually Innovate

AI-powered contact centers are no longer a novelty but necessary for organizations aiming for operational efficiency and customer satisfaction.

AI-powered contact centers are no longer a novelty but a necessity for organizations aiming for operational efficiency and customer satisfaction. However, merely implementing AI is not the end objective; the real challenge lies in continuously innovating your AI capabilities to sustain and enhance performance. Innovation isn't just about sporadic updates or incremental changes but a persistent, systematic effort to stay ahead of the curve.

Market conditions, consumer preferences, and a competitive landscape are dynamic elements that necessitate change. As AI algorithms are data-driven, the quality and scope of data are subject to these fluctuations. If your AI systems are not updated and trained on new data, they may become less effective or even obsolete. For instance, a machine learning model that was once proficient in managing customer queries may struggle if a new product line is introduced or customer inquiries increasingly become more nuanced.

AI is a fast-evolving field, with new techniques, algorithms, and paradigms frequently emerging. Techniques like transfer learning, GANs, and reinforcement learning continually push the boundaries of what is possible. Failing to keep pace with these advancements will inevitably lead to degrading service quality, operational efficiency, and competitiveness. On the other hand, adopting newer technologies can provide a significant advantage by enabling functionalities such as more accurate natural language understanding, personalized customer interactions, and automated problem-solving capabilities.

Plan to maintain compliance with legal frameworks and regulations. As rules evolve, so should your contact center's algorithms and data handling procedures to ensure you are not violating these regulations. This is particularly important in AI applications where data is a central asset, and non-compliance could lead to hefty fines or legal repercussions.

As more organizations adopt AI in their operations, the initial competitive advantage of merely having an AI-powered contact center diminishes. Hence, constant innovation is vital to keep your organization at the forefront of the competition. Innovation can happen at various levels, including user interface design, algorithmic efficiency, multi-channel support, and predictive analytics. Each enhancement not only adds value to the customer experience but also distinguishes your services from competitors who may be employing static or outdated AI technologies.

Consumer expectations are continuously rising, and the quality of customer service is often a key differentiator in the marketplace. Innovative AI features like sentiment analysis can help contact centers tailor their interactions to the customer's emotional state, leading to a more empathetic and effective service. Similarly, advancements in chatbot capabilities can resolve issues faster and provide a more human-like interaction, thereby elevating the overall customer experience.

The requisite for continuous innovation in AI-powered contact centers is not just theoretical but a pragmatic imperative for organizations seeking long-term success. It aligns with the dynamic nature of technology, market conditions, and consumer expectations. It serves to maintain compliance with evolving regulatory frameworks and sustains a competitive advantage.

Assess Your ACD

ACD systems are telephony technology at the heart of the contact center. The primary purpose of ACD systems is to streamline call handling, reduce wait times, and ensure a smooth customer experience. It plays a pivotal role in routing incoming calls to the most appropriate agents or departments, ensuring callers receive prompt and personalized service. To plan for the integration of AI, evaluating the existing ACD system's capabilities and limitations is imperative. Moreover, your assessment should consider whether AI can be your next-generation ACD.

An assessment aims to uncover opportunities where AI-powered solutions can enhance call routing, agent performance, and the overall customer experience. By thoroughly understanding the current ACD infrastructure, its strengths, and areas for improvement, organizations can strategically design an AI plan that aligns with their specific business goals, leveraging AI-driven innovations to unlock the full potential of their call center operations and deliver unparalleled service to customers. Here are the functions to assess:

1. Call Routing: When a customer initiates a call to your contact center, the ACD system answers the call and then routes it to the appropriate destination. The destination can be a specific agent, a group of agents with similar skills, or an interactive voice response (IVR) system for self-service options. Plan AI to analyze and understand the content of customer inquiries by

using NLP algorithms. AI can route the call to the best-suited agent by assessing the caller's intent and sentiment for personalized interactions.

2. Skill-Based Routing: Skill-based routing traditionally relies on predefined rules and criteria to direct incoming calls to the most appropriate agents with specific skills or expertise. Plan for AI to introduce more dynamic and sophisticated methods for call distribution. AI systems can continuously learn from each call, analyzing the outcomes and feedback to refine their routing decisions.

3. Queue Management: If all agents are busy, the ACD system places the call in a queue and plays a prerecorded message, music, or estimated wait time. Plan for AI-powered virtual agents, also known as chatbots, to handle routine and straightforward customer queries. This frees human agents to focus on more complex issues, reducing customer waiting times and increasing overall productivity.

4. Real-Time Monitoring and Reporting: Supervisors and managers can access real-time statistics and reports from the ACD system. Plan for AI to continuously evaluate agent performance, response times, successful issue resolution, customer satisfaction ratings, and other metrics. This enables AI to route calls to agents performing well in handling similar inquiries.

5. Integration with CRM Systems: Plan for AI-powered ACD systems to integrate with your CRM platforms to allow agents to access relevant customer information and call history, enabling personalized and efficient customer interactions.

Incorporating AI into an ACD can streamline call center operations, enhance customer satisfaction, and ultimately improve the overall efficiency and effectiveness of the customer support process. However, it's essential to strike a balance between AI and human interaction, ensuring that customers still have the option to speak with human agents when necessary.

B Assess Your IVR

IVRs are designed for self-service and respond to consumer requests for technical support, customer service, and sales assistance with omnichannel customer support, including calls, emails, website chat, and video. Customers who call your contact typically first interact with an IVR system. While IVRs and ACDs may both have call flow scripts, IVRs can access CRM systems to personalize the customer experience. This enables IVRs to provide self-service for customers with simple inquiries.

To understand your IVR, start with design documents, call scripts, and expected user experience. Document the IVR logic, including menu options, call routing, and prompts. The IVR logic will help plan the migration of a finite state dialog management model or provide the foundation for a more sophisticated probabilistic AI dialog management mode that offers natural and scalable ways to automate verbal conversation. Here are the steps to conduct an audit of your contact center IVR:

1. Understand All Flow and Routing Logic: Analyze the call flow and decision logic to understand how calls are routed through the IVR and directed to the appropriate departments or agents.

2. IVR Menu Navigation: Call into the IVR as a test customer and navigate through the menu options. Evaluate the clarity and simplicity of the menu prompts and assess if the options are logically organized.

3. Self-Service Functionality: Document the range of self-service choices offered by the IVR. Determine how many tasks customers can accomplish, such as checking their balances or tracking their orders, without needing assistance from an agent—plan for similar capabilities in your AI system.

4. Prompt Clarity and Tone: Evaluate the clarity and professionalism of IVR prompts. Verify that the voice prompts are easy to understand and use a tone appropriate for the organization's brand and image. Determine if TTS or NLG can provide equivalent clarity.

5. Language and Localization: If the contact center serves a multilingual or international customer base, check for language options and ensure that prompts are localized. Consider if multilingual conversational AI can dynamically translate to meet your business needs for generating responses in the customer's language.

6. Error Handling and Escalation: Test the IVR's error-handling capabilities by providing incorrect inputs or triggering error scenarios. Plan how the AI will handle such situations and if it offers appropriate escalation paths for callers with complex issues and transfers calls to live agents when necessary.

7. Integration with CRM: Evaluate how the IVR integrates with the contact center's CRM and other relevant data systems. Plan for how an AI system can access the same CRM system.

8. Performance Reporting: Review IVR performance reports, including call volumes, call duration, and IVR navigation patterns. Use this data as a benchmark and plan to improve performance with an AI system.

9. Customer Feedback: Gather feedback from customers who have interacted with the IVR. Analyze call recordings for customer sentiment and feedback on IVR usability.

10. Security and Data Privacy: Assess the IVR's security measures, ensuring customer data is protected and secure during interactions. AI security and data privacy will need to be equivalent.

Three Letter Acronyms & Lexicon

Artificial intelligence and the contact center industry are full of three or more letter acronyms (TLAs) and jargon that can overwhelm even the most knowledgeable individuals. This appendix summarizes TLAs and terms used in this book, but by no means is it a complete lexicon of all the terms used in either contact centers or the AI industry.

ABAC
Attribute-Based Access Control is a security model that determines access permissions based on attributes associated with users, resources, actions, and environmental conditions. ABAC allows for more fine-grained, context-sensitive access decisions than role-based access control, which relies solely on a user's role to grant or deny permissions. This approach enhances security and operational efficiency in contact centers by ensuring that agents, administrators, and other staff have access only to the specific information and functions that are necessary for their roles and tasks.

Accelerated Computing	Advances generative AI by significantly reducing training and inference times using specialized hardware such as graphics processing units (GPUs) and tensor processing units (TPUs). Generative models can leverage parallel processing to accelerate computations and efficiently handle complex tasks. This acceleration enables researchers and practitioners to train larger models, explore more sophisticated architectures, and achieve higher-quality outputs in various generative AI applications, ranging from image synthesis to natural language generation.
ACW	After-Call Work is a set of necessary tasks that need to be completed after an agent interacts with the customer. These include updating the system, logging the reason for contact and outcome, updating colleagues, and scheduling follow-up actions. ACW varies across different customer queries and resolution requests. There is no predetermined yardstick for the duration of ACW. However, it is a metric that impacts average handle time (AHT) and must be closely tracked.
ADC	Automatic Call Distributor is a telephony system that manages incoming calls and routes them to specific agents or departments within a contact center based on predefined rules and criteria. These criteria can include agent availability, skill sets, or other factors that contribute to efficient call handling and improved customer service. An ACD optimizes resource allocation in the contact center, thereby reducing wait times for customers and enhancing the overall efficiency and effectiveness of the operation.

Agent Assist	Refers to the utilization of artificial intelligence and other advanced technologies to support human customer service agents in their tasks, including call handling, problem-solving, and customer engagement. These systems typically offer real-time guidance, automated responses, and contextual information to help agents efficiently address customer inquiries and concerns. The ultimate goal is to enhance the customer experience by expediting resolution times, improving accuracy, and allowing human agents to focus on more complex or emotionally nuanced interactions.
AGI	Artificial General Intelligence (AGI) or strong AI represents a theoretical form of AI that proposes solving any number of hypothetical tasks using generalized human cognitive abilities. In theory, AGI will be able to understand, learn, and apply knowledge across a wide range of functions, similar to humans. The ultimate goal of AGI is to replicate the broad range of human cognitive abilities called common-sense reasoning. AGI research is still evolving, and researchers are divided on the approach and timelines to bring it to reality.
AHT	Average Handle Time is a contact center metric used to measure the average duration of one transaction. It usually starts from the customer beginning the interaction and covers hold time, talk time, and any other related tasks during the conversation.
AI	Artificial Intelligence refers to developing and implementing computer systems that can perform tasks typically requiring human intelligence, such as learning, problem-solving, and decision-making. Examples of AI include understanding human text and speech and detecting and translating languages.

AI Act	A regulatory framework proposed by the European Union to govern the development, deployment, and use of artificial intelligence systems within the EU. It aims to ensure AI's ethical and trustworthy use while promoting innovation and competitiveness. The Act introduces requirements for high-risk AI systems, including transparency, accountability, and human oversight. It establishes a comprehensive framework for AI governance and market surveillance to protect the rights and safety of individuals.
AI Domain	The range of AI technologies specifically tailored for customer service environments, including but not limited to natural language processing (NLP), machine learning algorithms, and automated decision-making systems. These technologies are designed to assist or automate various functions within the contact center, such as customer engagement, routing, and analytics.
AI Domain Description	Detailed explanations or specifications of the specific AI domains that refer to particular areas or fields of knowledge where AI techniques and technologies are applied to solve certain problems or address specific challenges. Domain descriptions provide a deeper understanding of the AI technologies, their applications, and how they fit into your contact center setup. Domain descriptions could include information about the capabilities of AI technologies within the chosen domain, their benefits, potential use cases, and considerations for implementation, as well as define the scope and context of your AI application.
AI Project Lifecycle	Outlines the sequential phases involved in planning, developing, deploying, and maintaining AI technologies within a customer service environment. The lifecycle typically starts with problem identification and requirement gathering, followed by the design, development, and testing of the AI solutions, and culminates in deployment, monitoring, and ongoing optimization. Each phase has its own set of methodologies, best practices, and metrics for success, ensuring that the AI initiative aligns with the contact center's broader operational and business objectives.

Algorithm	Algorithms are a set of rules a computer follows while executing operations. Algorithms tell a computer how to act in various situations. Combining multiple algorithms allows applications to perform more sophisticated tasks without human intervention. For example, a chatbot can use algorithms to suggest products based on a shopper's purchase history or route customers to a specific human agent whose specialty best matches the incoming question.
ANN	Artificial Neural Networks are biologically inspired computational networks that simulate the human brain processes. ANNs consist of interconnected nodes, called artificial neurons or units, organized into layers which include an input layer, one or more hidden layers, and an output layer. ANNs can learn from data by adjusting the weights and biases of the connections between neurons, enabling them to process complex information, recognize patterns, and make predictions or decisions. ANNs have been successfully applied to various tasks, such as image recognition, natural language processing, and time series prediction.
Anonymization	The process of irreversibly transforming or removing personally identifiable information from a dataset so that individuals cannot be readily identified. Unlike redaction or data masking, which may allow for the possibility of re-identification, anonymization aims to eliminate that risk entirely. In the context of contact centers, anonymization is often used to protect customer privacy and ensure compliance with data protection regulations while still allowing for the analysis and utilization of the data for operational improvements and insights. See Redaction.
AR	Augmented Reality is an interactive experience that enhances the real world with computer-generated perceptual information. Using software, apps, and hardware such as AR glasses, augmented reality overlays digital content onto real-life environments and objects.

ASA	Average Speed of Answer is a KPI commonly used in contact centers to measure the average time it takes for incoming calls to be answered by an agent. The metric is usually calculated by dividing the total wait time for answered calls by the total number of answered calls within a specific time period. ASA serves as an important gauge for assessing the efficiency and responsiveness of a contact center, with shorter ASA times generally indicating better customer service and resource allocation.
ASR	Automated Speech Recognition, also known as speech recognition, computer speech recognition, or speech-to-text, enables a program to process human speech into a written format. ASR uses algorithms and models to analyze and transcribe audio signals into textual representations. ASR applications are in various domains, including voice assistants, transcription services, call centers, and language processing, enabling efficient and accurate conversion of spoken words into text data.
Avatar	A digital representation or embodiment of an entity, often a person or a character that interacts with users in virtual environments or through digital platforms. Avatars can be visual representations in the form of animated characters or graphical icons, or they can be voice-based representations in the case of virtual assistants or chatbots. They are designed to simulate human-like behavior and engage in conversational interactions, providing personalized and interactive experiences for users.
Bias	When an algorithm shows prejudice in favor of or against one thing, person, or group compared with another, usually in a way considered unfair. Bias is a systematic error that occurs because of incorrect algorithm assumptions. For example, if the algorithm only had information on an apple and no other fruit, it would assume that an apple is the only type of fruit. Because of bias, AI tools like chatbots are more likely to give specific responses over others, even when those answers may be false.

Big Data	An enormous data set too large to process with traditional computing. AI software can analyze these large databases through data mining to identify patterns and draw conclusions. Access to big data allows AI solutions to respond with more intelligence and deliver more human-like interactions.
Burst Test	A method used to evaluate the strength and performance of materials or products under high-pressure conditions. It involves subjecting the material or product to increasing internal pressure until it reaches its bursting point. This test helps determine the maximum pressure the material can withstand before failure, providing valuable insights into its durability, reliability, and safety in real-world applications.
BYOC	Bring Your Own Carrier refers to the practice of allowing organizations to select and integrate their own telecommunications service providers rather than being limited to the options offered by the data center. This enables greater flexibility and customization of services, such as voice, data, and internet connectivity, according to the organization's specific needs and preferences. BYOC can offer benefits like cost savings, improved performance, and the ability to leverage existing relationships with carriers while still utilizing the data center's infrastructure for other services.
CCaaS	Contact Center as a Service is a cloud-based customer experience solution that allows companies to utilize contact center capabilities without the need to own, host, or maintain the underlying infrastructure. CCaaS providers offer a range of functionalities, including but not limited to call routing, customer interaction analytics, workforce optimization, and omnichannel support. This model offers scalability, flexibility, and cost-efficiency, enabling organizations to focus on improving customer service while reducing capital expenditure and operational costs.

CCP	Concurrent Call Path refers to the number of simultaneous voice conversations that a telecommunication system, often within a contact center, can handle at any given time. This metric is crucial for determining the capacity and scalability of a phone system, dictating how many callers can be accommodated without experiencing busy signals or dropped calls. Understanding and planning for the appropriate number of concurrent call paths is vital for ensuring efficient operations, optimal customer experience, and cost-effective utilization of telecommunication resources.
CCPA	The California Consumer Privacy Act is a state-level data protection law that went into effect on January 1, 2020, granting California residents enhanced privacy rights and consumer protection regarding their personal data. The legislation provides individuals with the right to know what data is being collected about them, the right to delete personal data held by businesses, and the right to opt out of the sale of their data. Companies that do business in California and meet certain criteria are required to comply with the CCPA, and non-compliance can result in substantial fines and legal penalties.
CES	Customer Effort Score is a single-item metric that measures how much effort a customer has to exert to resolve an issue, a request, or a question.
Chatbot	An AI program designed to simulate human conversation and provide automated responses to users. It utilizes natural language processing techniques to understand and interpret user input, allowing it to engage in interactive conversations. Chatbots are employed in various applications, such as customer support, virtual assistants, and information retrieval, offering a convenient and efficient way to interact with computer systems through conversation.
ChatGPT	An NLP tool driven by AI technology that allows human-like conversations. The language model can answer questions and assist you with tasks like composing emails, essays, and code.

Classification	A fundamental task in machine learning that involves assigning a category or label to a given input data point based on its characteristics. In other words, classification is a supervised learning method that allows machines to learn how to classify new instances into a pre-defined set of categories based on the features present in the data.
CML	Continuous Machine Learning helps with continuous improvements. CML's most basic application is in circumstances where the data distributions remain constant, but the data is continuous. It automates your Machine Learning process, such as model training and evaluation, comparing trials throughout your project history, and monitoring dataset changes. If you are familiar with Netflix's recommender system, which has an "Up Next" feature that plays shows similar to the ones you've recently watched, then you have seen a CML model in action.
CMS	The Call Management System is a software solution designed to collect and analyze real-time and historical data related to contact center operations. It enables organizations to monitor key performance indicators (KPIs), such as call volumes, handling times, and service level metrics, providing insights that help optimize agent productivity and customer experience. Through its suite of reporting and analytical tools, CMS assists in resource planning, performance evaluation, and strategic decision-making in the contact center environment.
CNN	Convolutional Neural Network is a class of deep neural networks primarily used in the processing and analysis of visual data, such as images and videos. The architecture is designed to automatically and adaptively learn spatial hierarchies of features through its multiple layers, which include convolutional layers, pooling layers, and fully connected layers. CNNs have become the de facto standard for tasks like image recognition, object detection, and various other computer vision applications due to their ability to handle high-dimensional input data and produce accurate results efficiently.

Conversational AI	The use of AI technologies to enable natural language interactions between humans and machines. It involves the development of intelligent systems capable of understanding and generating human-like speech or text. Conversational AI encompasses various technologies, such as chatbots, virtual assistants, and voice recognition systems, aiming to provide seamless and interactive communication experiences for users across different platforms and applications.
Covariate shift	A type of drift in which the data features have changed but not necessarily the model performance. It occurs when the distribution of input data shifts between the training environment and the live environment. A shift can occur gradually over time or suddenly after deployment. In both cases, the issue will have an adverse effect on the accuracy of the model.
CPU	Central Processing Unit, called the "central" or "main" processor, is a complex set of electronic circuitries running the machine's operating system and apps. It is the primary component of a computer that acts as its "control center."
CRM	Customer Relationship Management system is a technology platform that centralizes, automates, and systematizes interactions between a business and its customers. It serves as a repository for customer information, purchase history, service interactions, and other relevant data, thereby enabling organizations to manage relationships, identify opportunities, and optimize customer experiences.
CSAT	Customer Satisfaction is a commonly used metric indicating customer satisfaction with a company's products or services. It's measured through customer feedback and expressed as a percentage (100% would be excellent – 0% would be abysmal).
Data Drift	The phenomenon where the statistical properties of the target variable, which the machine learning model is trying to predict, change over time in unforeseen ways, causing the model's performance to degrade. This occurs when the data used for training no longer represents the current environment where the model is deployed, leading to inaccuracies and predictive errors.

Data Labeling	Data labeling refers to the process of annotating raw data, such as images, text, or audio, with informative tags or labels to create a labeled dataset. These annotations serve as ground truth, enabling supervised learning algorithms to train on this data to recognize patterns, make predictions, or classify new, unlabeled data. The quality and accuracy of the data labeling process are crucial for the performance and reliability of the AI models trained on such datasets.
DBMS	Database Management Systems are designed to store, manage, and manipulate databases, which can include various types of data such as text, numbers, multimedia, and more. The DBMS provides an interface between the database and the users or the application programs, ensuring that the data is consistently organized and remains easily accessible. Functionality generally includes data retrieval, insertion, update, and deletion, as well as various administrative operations like backup, security, and data integrity.
Deep Learning	A specialized subset of machine learning that mimics the neural networks of the human brain to process data and create patterns for decision-making. It utilizes multiple layers of artificial neural networks to automatically learn to perform tasks without human intervention, essentially training itself by analyzing various forms of data. Deep learning techniques are particularly effective for complex tasks like image and speech recognition, natural language processing, and autonomous driving, often outperforming traditional machine learning algorithms in these domains.
Dialogue Logic	The systematic rules and principles that govern the flow of conversation and interaction between participants in a dialogue. It encompasses the logical structure and coherence of the dialogue, including the organization of topics, the sequencing of turns, and the rules for exchanging information and responses. Dialogue logic aims to ensure meaningful and effective communication by establishing guidelines for logical reasoning, turn-taking, and the coherent exchange of ideas.

Dialogue Management	The process of orchestrating and controlling the flow of conversation between a computer system and a user. It involves coordinating various components, such as natural language understanding, dialogue policies, and system responses to enable effective communication. Dialogue management systems utilize state tracking, user intent recognition, and response generation to maintain context, handle user requests, and provide appropriate and coherent system responses throughout the dialogue.
DID	Direct Inward Dialing refers to a service allowing a company to allocate individual phone numbers to specific lines, extensions, or employees without requiring separate physical phone lines. These numbers are mapped to existing phone lines via a Private Branch Exchange (PBX) system, enabling direct, targeted routing of incoming calls. DID facilitates efficient call management and personalization, allowing for streamlined internal and external communications without the need for a centralized reception or switchboard.
DL	Deep Learning is a subset of machine learning that utilizes artificial neural networks with multiple layers to learn and extract high-level representations from complex data. Deep learning models can recognize intricate patterns in pictures, text, sounds, and other data to produce accurate insights and predictions. Deep learning methods automate tasks that typically require human intelligence, such as transcribing a sound file into text.
Dynamic AI	The use of artificial intelligence systems that can adapt and evolve in real-time based on changing environments or data inputs. It involves the ability of AI models to update their internal representations, decision-making processes, or behavior dynamically. Dynamic AI enables systems to respond effectively to new information, handle varying conditions, and improve their performance over time, making them more flexible, robust, and capable of learning from dynamic and evolving situations.

Dynamic AL	Dynamic Active Learning is an approach used in machine learning and data annotation where the selection of informative samples for labeling is adapted dynamically during the learning process. It involves iteratively updating the sample selection criteria based on the current state of the model and the available labeled data. Dynamic AL aims to maximize the learning efficiency by prioritizing the labeling of samples that are expected to provide the most significant improvement to the model's performance, leading to faster convergence and reduced annotation efforts.
EQ	Emotional Quotients, or Emotional Intelligence (EI), acquire data through real-world data, speech science, and deep learning algorithms. The data is processed and compared to other data points to detect important emotions like fear and joy. After finding the correct emotion, the computer interprets it and what it might mean in each situation. Emotional Intelligence becomes more adept at recognizing the subtleties of human communication as the emotion database expands.
F1 Score	A metric used to evaluate the performance of binary classification models, offering a balance between precision and recall. It is calculated as the harmonic mean of the precision and recall, where precision is the number of true positive results divided by the number of all positive results, and recall is the number of true positive results divided by the number of positive results that should have been returned. The F1 Score ranges from 0 to 1, where a score of 1 indicates perfect precision and recall, and a score of 0 indicates the worst possible performance.
FAQ	Frequently Asked Questions generally provide information on frequent questions or concerns. They are often organized in articles, websites, email lists, and online forums where common questions tend to recur—for instance, posts or queries by new users related to common knowledge gaps.

FCR	First Contact Resolution is a metric used to measure customer inquiries or problems resolved on the first call or contact with a representative or agent. FCR is one of the most commonly measured metrics in the contact center industry. Ideally, the FCR definition means no repeat calls or contacts are required from the initial call or contact reason from a customer perspective.
Feedback Data	In predictive machines, feedback data refers to the information or evaluations provided to the model after making predictions or decisions. It is used to assess the performance and accuracy of the model's outputs. Feedback data can include ground truth labels, user ratings, error metrics, or other forms of feedback that help refine and improve the model's predictions through iterative learning processes.
FL	Federated Learning is a machine learning approach that allows a model to be trained across multiple decentralized devices or servers holding local data samples without exchanging them. Instead of sending raw data to a centralized server, local models are trained on each device or server. The model updates are then sent to a central server, aggregating them to produce a global model. This approach aims to improve privacy, security, and efficiency, as sensitive data remains on the local device and only relevant model information is communicated.
Form-Based Model	A type of AI model designed to interact with users through pre-defined form-based inputs and responses. It typically involves structured input formats such as fillable forms or questionnaires, where users provide specific information or answer predefined questions. AI form-based models utilize natural language processing and pattern-matching techniques to understand and process the user's input, generating appropriate responses or actions based on the form data provided. These models are commonly used in applications like surveys, data collection, and automated customer support.

The Fourth Industrial Era	Also known as the fourth revolution in industry because it brings about a significant change in how industries function, much like the previous industrial revolutions. It uses sophisticated algorithms and computing capabilities to automate processes, enhance decision-making, and improve efficiency and productivity in various sectors. Like the earlier industrial revolutions, AI's influence on industries is predicted to be profound and disruptive, transforming society's landscape.
FSM	Finite State Machines, also known as Finite State AL models, are computational models that consist of a finite number of states and transitions between those states. Each state represents a specific condition or configuration of the system, and the transitions represent the actions or events that cause the system to move from one state to another. Finite State AI models are often used in decision-making processes or simple rule-based systems, where the current state and the input received determine the behavior of the AI.
GAI	Generative AI is a class of AI techniques that focuses on generating new content or data rather than just analyzing or classifying existing information. It involves training models to learn patterns and structures from existing data and to use that knowledge to generate new, original content. Generative AI has applications in various domains, such as image synthesis, text generation, music composition, and even video generation, enabling the creation of realistic and novel outputs.
GAN	Generative Adversarial Networks are a type of neural network architecture consisting of two components, a generator and a discriminator, that compete against each other to generate realistic data samples.

GDPR	General Data Protection Regulation is a comprehensive data protection law enacted by the European Union in 2018, replacing the Data Protection Directive of 1995. It aims to standardize data protection laws across EU member states and to protect the privacy and personal data of EU citizens, including the control and processing of such data. Organizations that handle personal data, irrespective of their geographical location, are obligated to comply with GDPR provisions, with penalties for non-compliance that can be as high as 4% of the company's annual global revenue or €20 million, whichever is greater.
GPT	Generative Pre-trained Transformers are a family of neural network models that uses the transformer architecture and is a crucial advancement in generative AI applications such as ChatGPT, with the ability to create human-like text and content and conversationally answer questions.
GPU	Graphics Processing Unit is a hardware component that accelerates machine learning models' training and inference processes. GPUs excel at performing parallel computations, making them highly efficient for training deep neural networks and processing large datasets. With their massive parallelism and high memory bandwidth, GPUs have become a crucial tool in AI, enabling faster model training and improved performance in various AI applications.
Hallucination	The phenomenon where artificial intelligence systems, particularly generative models, produce imaginative or unrealistic outputs, diverging from the intended or expected results. It can occur when AI models generate highly creative content that lacks fidelity to the real world. AI hallucinations can be observed in various applications, such as image synthesis or text generation, where the models generate outputs that exhibit imaginative elements or distortions not present in the training data.

HIPAA	Health Insurance Portability and Accountability Act of 1996 (HIPAA or the Kennedy–Kassebaum Act) is a United States Act of Congress enacted by the 104th United States Congress and signed into law by President Bill Clinton on August 21, 1996. It modernized the flow of healthcare information and stipulated how personally identifiable information (PII) maintained by the healthcare and healthcare insurance industries should be protected from fraud and theft.
Hyperparameter	A configuration variable that is external to the model and whose value is set prior to the commencement of the training process. Unlike model parameters, which are learned directly from the training data, hyperparameters are not learned from the data but are set a priori to guide the learning process. Common examples of hyperparameters include the learning rate in gradient boosting, the regularization term in logistic regression, and the number of hidden layers in a neural network.
IHT	Interaction Handling Time refers to the duration it takes to handle a customer interaction or query from start to finish in a contact center or customer service environment. It includes the time spent on activities like greeting the customer, gathering information, providing assistance, resolving issues, and concluding the interaction. Monitoring and minimizing IHT is crucial for improving operational efficiency and customer satisfaction in contact center operations.
Inference	The process of using a trained model to make predictions or draw conclusions from new, unseen data. It involves applying the learned patterns and relationships from the training phase to make informed decisions on input data. During inference, the model takes in input data, processes it, and produces the desired output, such as classification labels or regression values, based on its learned knowledge.

Input Data	In predictive machines, input data refers to the information or features provided to the machine learning model for making predictions or decisions. It is the data that the model uses as input to learn patterns and relationships. The input data can vary depending on the specific problem. Still, it typically includes relevant attributes, variables, or measurements that are expected to influence the outcome or prediction made by the model.
Intent	The goal a human has when interacting with a machine. For instance, when a customer asks a chatbot about the location of their package, an AI tool would recognize the user's intent as requesting information about their order status. Identifying a user's intent enables a chatbot to generate specific responses tailored to a person's unique needs.
IVA	Intelligent Virtual Assistant is a software program or application that uses artificial intelligence and natural language processing to interact with users and provide them with assistance or information. IVAs are designed to simulate human-like conversations and can understand and respond to user queries or commands. They are commonly used in customer service, virtual agents, and chatbot applications to provide automated support and enhance user experiences.
IVR	Interactive Voice Response is an automated telephony system that interacts with callers through voice or keypad inputs. It uses pre-recorded voice prompts and menu options to guide callers through various options and route them to the appropriate department or information. IVRs are commonly used in customer support, call centers, and phone-based services to handle a high volume of calls efficiently and provide self-service options to callers.

JSON	JavaScript Object Notation is a lightweight data-interchange format that is easy for humans to read and write and easy for machines to parse and generate. It is based on a subset of the JavaScript language. It is often used for transmitting structured data over a network, commonly in web applications, to exchange data between a client and a server.
KB	Knowledge Base is a set of data available for a program to access to perform a task or give a response. The larger the knowledge base an AI application has access to, the more comprehensive the range of problems it can solve. AI programs can only pull from the knowledge base they have access to.
K-Fold Cross-Validation	A statistical technique used in machine learning to assess the performance of a predictive model. In this method, the original dataset is randomly partitioned into 'k' equally-sized or nearly equal subsamples; of these, a single subsample is retained as the validation set, and the remaining 'k-1' subsamples are used as the training set. The cross-validation process is then repeated 'k' times, each time with a different subsample serving as the validation set, and the model's performance is averaged over all 'k' runs to provide a more robust evaluation.
KPI	Key Performance Indicators are metrics used to assess the performance and effectiveness of a contact center in delivering customer service and achieving business goals. Common KPIs include average handling time (AHT), which measures the average duration of customer interactions; first call resolution (FCR), which tracks the percentage of customer issues resolved in a single contact; and customer satisfaction (CSAT) scores, which gauge customer satisfaction with the service received. Monitoring and improving these KPIs can help organizations enhance operational efficiency, customer experience, and overall contact center performance.

LLM	Large Language Models are deep-learning algorithms that recognize and generate content after training on massive amounts of data. The larger the dataset is, the more effective a language model will be at understanding, translating, and predicting text. LLMs utilize deep learning techniques like transformer architectures to generate human-like text and understand natural language. LLMs can perform various language-related tasks, including text generation, translation, summarization, and question answering, and have been influential in advancing natural language processing applications.
Load Test	A type of performance testing that evaluates the behavior and performance of a system under specific anticipated loads or stress conditions. It involves subjecting the system to simulated user activity or traffic to measure its response time, throughput, and scalability. Load tests help identify potential bottlenecks, performance limitations, or areas of improvement in the system, ensuring it can handle expected loads effectively and maintain optimal performance.
LSTM	Long Short-Term Memory is a type of recurrent neural network (RNN) architecture specifically designed to address the vanishing gradient problem and capture long-term dependencies in sequential data. It utilizes memory cells, input, and forget gates to regulate the flow of information, making it capable of learning and retaining information over long sequences. LSTMs have proven effective in various tasks involving sequential data, such as speech recognition, machine translation, and sentiment analysis.

ML	Machine Learning is a branch of artificial intelligence that focuses on developing algorithms and models that allow computers to learn from and make predictions or decisions based on data. It involves using statistical techniques and algorithms to automatically enable computers to identify patterns and extract meaningful insights from large datasets. Machine learning algorithms can adapt and optimize their predictions or actions over time by iteratively improving their performance through data exposure.
Model	The model defines the relationship between the input data, which we call features, and what the model is trying to predict, called the labeled data. The data that is labeled is evidence. Labeled data could be the square footage of a house or the total sales in a day. It's the evidence that gets collected and submitted. The models then train with these datasets; the more data you give a model, the better it predicts over time.
NCP	Non-Player Characters are characters in video games or virtual environments controlled by the game's artificial intelligence rather than a human player. They are designed to interact with the player or other characters, often serving specific roles within the game's storyline, quests, or gameplay mechanics. NPCs can range from friendly allies to neutral bystanders or hostile enemies, providing a dynamic and immersive experience for the player.
NER	Named Entity Relationships is an NLP method that extracts information from text, detecting and categorizing pertinent information known as "named entities." Named entities refer to the key subjects of a piece of text, such as names, locations, companies, events, and products, as well as themes, topics, times, monetary values, and percentages.

Neural Networks	A class of machine learning models inspired by the structure and function of the human brain. They consist of interconnected nodes, called neurons, organized into layers. These networks learn from data by adjusting the weights and biases of the connections between neurons, enabling them to capture complex patterns and relationships in the data and make predictions or decisions. Neural networks have shown remarkable performance in various domains, including image recognition, natural language processing, and pattern classification.
NLG	Natural Language Generation is a field of AI that focuses on generating human-like natural language text or speech based on structured data or other input forms. It is the opposite of NLU transforming structured information into coherent and understandable human spoken words mimicking natural language patterns and conventions. NLU can be combined with other AI technologies, such as natural language understanding and dialogue systems, to create interactive conversational agents or chatbots.
NLP	Natural language processing has existed for over 50 years and has roots in linguistics. In AI, NLP is a program's ability to interpret written and spoken human language, allowing computers to understand text and spoken words like human beings, including their tone and intent. NLP combines computational linguistics for rule-based modeling of human language with statistical, machine learning, and deep learning models. There are two main phases to natural language processing: data preprocessing involves preparing and "cleaning" text data for machines to be able to analyze it, and algorithm development. NLP enables chatbots to detect customer sentiment, including determining if the customer is frustrated, complaining, or simply completing a request.

NLU	Natural Language Understanding is a branch of AI focusing on the interaction between computers and human language. It is a subfield of NLP that enables computers to understand, interpret, and derive meaning from language similarly to humans. NLU involves developing algorithms, models, and systems to process and comprehend natural language inputs, such as text or speech, extract relevant information, understand the context, and derive the intended meaning.
NPS	Net Promoter Score is a metric used in contact centers to measure customer loyalty and satisfaction. It is based on the question, "On a scale of 0 to 10, how likely are you to recommend our company/service to a friend or colleague?" Customers are then categorized into promoters (rating 9-10), passives (rating 7-8), or detractors (rating 0-6). The NPS is calculated by subtracting the percentage of detractors from the percentage of promoters, providing an overall indication of customer sentiment and loyalty.
PBX	Private Branch eXchange is a small version of a telephone company's central office. PBXs can handle both inbound and outbound calls but are more flexible and can be programmed to meet your business requirements.
PoC	Proof of Concept (PoC) serves as a preliminary demonstration that illustrates the feasibility of the proposed artificial intelligence technologies: chatbots, natural language processing engines, or advanced routing algorithms. It is essentially a small-scale, often limited-scope project that aims to validate the technical and operational viability of the AI solution within the contact center environment. Your business can identify potential barriers by successfully executing a PoC, assess system integration needs, and gauge overall effectiveness before committing to full-scale implementation.

PoC	Proof of Concept is an experimental demonstration designed to ascertain the feasibility and practicality of a proposed idea, project, or system. It serves as an initial stage where key technical and operational aspects are tested, but without the requirement to be fully functional or comprehensive. By validating the core mechanisms and potential benefits, a PoC helps decision-makers assess whether the idea is worth investing in for full-scale development.
Prediction Machines	Computational systems or algorithms designed to make predictions or forecasts based on available data. They utilize machine learning and statistical techniques to analyze patterns, correlations, and trends in data and generate predictions about future outcomes. Prediction machines have diverse applications across industries, including finance, healthcare, weather forecasting, and sales forecasting, providing valuable insights for decision-making and planning.
Predictive Analytics	A machine learning technique to predict future outcomes or behaviors using historical data and statistical algorithms. It involves analyzing past patterns and trends to make informed predictions about future events, behaviors, or probabilities. By leveraging data-driven insights, predictive analytics enables organizations to anticipate outcomes, make proactive decisions, and optimize strategies across various business, finance, marketing, and healthcare domains.
Primary Data	Original, unmediated data collected directly from the environment, subjects, or processes under study, specifically for the purpose of training, validating, or testing the algorithm. Primary data is raw and closely represents the attributes or variables that the algorithm aims to analyze or predict. The quality, reliability, and appropriateness of the primary data source are critical factors in determining the accuracy and efficacy of the resulting AI model. See Secondary Data.

Probabilistic Model	A mathematical framework used to represent uncertainty and randomness in data. It assigns probabilities to different outcomes or events based on available information or prior knowledge. By capturing the probabilistic relationships between variables, a probabilistic model enables reasoning, prediction, and inference about uncertain quantities and allows for probabilistic reasoning in decision-making processes.
RBAC	Role-Based Access Control is a security framework in which permissions and access to resources are granted based on predefined roles within the organization. Under this model, each role is associated with a specific set of permissions and access rights, which are then inherited by users assigned to that role. RBAC simplifies the management of access controls by allowing administrators to manage roles rather than individual users, thus making it easier to enforce security policies and manage personnel changes within the contact center.
Redaction	The process of removing or obscuring sensitive or confidential information from a document, audio file, or other data source before it is published, shared, or archived. The primary objective is to protect individual privacy, comply with regulations, or meet security requirements while still making the non-sensitive portions of the information available for use. In the context of contact centers, redaction is often employed to ensure that customer data and interactions are compliant with privacy laws, such as the GDPR or HIPAA. See Anonymization.

Regression Testing	A software testing technique to ensure that recent changes or modifications to a system have not introduced new defects or caused unintended side effects in previously functioning features. It involves retesting the existing test cases to verify the system's behavior and confirm that it still operates as expected after the changes. Regression testing helps maintain the stability and reliability of the software by catching any regressions or issues that might have been introduced during the development process.
Reinforcement Learning	A machine learning paradigm that involves an agent learning to make sequential decisions through interaction with an environment. The agent receives feedback through rewards or punishments based on its actions, allowing it to learn optimal strategies through trial and error. Maximizing cumulative rewards over time, the agent aims to find the best course of action in a given environment, making reinforcement learning well-suited for tasks such as game-playing, robotics, and autonomous decision-making.
Request Technologies	Request Technologies combined with NLG responses allow customers to interact in two-way conversations between the customer and an AI-powered prediction machine.
RLHF	Reinforcement Learning from Human Feedback is an approach in ML where an agent learns from feedback provided by human trainers to improve decision-making capabilities. It involves a human providing evaluations or demonstrations to guide the agent's learning process. RLHF leverages the expertise of human trainers to accelerate the learning process and enhance the performance of the agent in complex and dynamic environments.

RNN	Recurrent Neural Networks are a class of artificial neural networks designed to process sequential data by utilizing feedback connections. They can retain information from previous inputs in their hidden states, allowing them to capture temporal dependencies and contextual information. RNNs have found applications in various tasks such as natural language processing, speech recognition, and time series analysis, where the order and sequence of the data play a crucial role in the analysis and prediction.
ROI	Return on Investment is a financial metric used to evaluate the profitability and effectiveness of an investment, expressed as a percentage. It is calculated by dividing the net gain obtained from the investment by its initial cost and then multiplying the result by 100. ROI serves as a key indicator for businesses and individuals to assess the value generated by an investment relative to its cost, aiding in decision-making processes for future investments or resource allocations. See TCO.
Rule-Based Systems	Rule-Based Systems are a type of knowledge-based system that utilizes a set of predefined rules to make decisions or perform actions. These systems consist of a rule base containing a collection of if-then statements or conditions and an inference engine that applies these rules to process input data and generate output. Rule-Based Systems are commonly used in domains where expert knowledge can be explicitly represented, such as in expert systems, decision support systems, and diagnostic systems.
Secondary Data	A dataset not originally collected for the specific purpose of training, validating, or testing the algorithm in question but repurposed for these functions. Secondary data may have been gathered for other research objectives, administrative records, or prior analyses and is often aggregated, processed, or summarized. While secondary data sources offer the advantages of time and cost savings, their utility in AI applications may be limited by issues related to data relevance, consistency, and completeness. See Primary Data.

Semi-Structured Data	Data that falls between structured and unstructured data, containing elements of both. It is characterized by its lack of a rigid structure, but it does have tags, hierarchies, or other markers that help in categorizing and organizing the information. Formats like XML, JSON, and YAML files are common examples of semi-structured data, where the data is not in a tabular form but contains tags or keys to provide some level of structure and context. See Structured Data, Unstructured Data.
Semi-Supervised Learning	A machine learning paradigm that combines supervised and unsupervised learning elements. It involves training a model using a small amount of labeled data and a larger amount of unlabeled data. The labeled data helps the model learn from explicit examples, while the unlabeled data aids in discovering underlying patterns and structures in the data. This approach is useful when labeled data is scarce or expensive to obtain, allowing for more efficient and cost-effective training of models.
SIP	Session Initiation Protocol is a telecommunications protocol widely used for initiating, maintaining, and terminating real-time sessions that involve voice, video, messaging, and other communications applications and services. It functions at the application layer of the Internet Protocol (IP) suite and plays a pivotal role in the control of multimedia communication sessions in Voice over IP (VoIP) networks. By establishing, modifying, or terminating multimedia sessions, SIP serves as a fundamental protocol in the architecture of various forms of internet telephony and converged IP-based communication systems.

SLA	Service Level Agreement is a contractual document that delineates the standards of service a client can expect from a service provider, specifying metrics like response times, resolution times, and availability rates. These agreements serve as a formal understanding between both parties, delineating the scope and quality of the services to be provided. SLAs are critical for establishing mutual accountability and setting clear performance benchmarks, often incorporating penalties for non-compliance and outlining remediation procedures.
Slots	Slots are variables or placeholders used to store information during the processing of input data. Slots are associated with specific states in the model and can be filled with different values as the AI system encounters and processes various inputs. By utilizing slots, the AI model can retain context and make decisions based on the accumulated information within the states.
SLU	Spoken Language Understanding is a subfield of natural language processing (NLP) that focuses on interpreting and understanding spoken language by machines. It involves analyzing and processing spoken utterances to extract meaning, intent, and context. SLU techniques are used in applications such as voice assistants, speech recognition systems, and automated call centers to enable machines to comprehend and respond to human speech effectively.
SMPC	Secure Multi-Party Computation is a cryptographic technique that allows multiple parties to collaboratively compute a function over their respective inputs while keeping those inputs private. In essence, SMPC enables computations to occur without requiring any party to reveal their confidential data to others, thus ensuring data privacy and security. This methodology is particularly useful in scenarios where sensitive data must be analyzed collectively without exposure, such as in privacy-preserving medical research, financial services, or secure voting systems.

SMS	Short Message Service is a communication protocol for sending short text messages between mobile devices. It enables users to exchange text-based messages, typically limited to 160 characters per message, over cellular networks. SMS is widely used for personal and business communications, providing a quick and convenient way to send messages between mobile devices.
SQL	Structured Query Language is a domain-specific language used for managing and manipulating relational databases. SQL enables tasks such as querying data, updating data, inserting data, and deleting data from a database, as well as creating and modifying schemas that describe the structure of the database. It serves as the standard interface for various DBMS, including proprietary and open-source solutions.
Static AI	Artificial intelligence systems or models trained on fixed, pre-existing datasets that do not dynamically adapt or update based on real-time information or feedback. These AI models operate based on a predetermined set of rules and patterns and do not actively learn or evolve from new data. Static AI is commonly used in scenarios where the underlying data is relatively stable, and there is no need for continuous learning or adaptation.
Stress Test	A type of performance testing that evaluates the behavior and stability of a system under extreme or peak load conditions. It aims to identify a system's breaking point or maximum capacity and assess its response to heavy traffic or stress factors. By simulating high user volumes or intensive workloads, stress tests help uncover performance bottlenecks, resource limitations, or system failures, providing insights into the system's robustness and resilience.

Structured Data	Data organized into a specific format or schema, such as tables, rows, and columns, which makes it easily searchable and analyzable by computer algorithms. Common examples include relational databases, where data is stored in tables, or CSV files, where values are separated by commas. The explicit structure and organization of this type of data facilitate efficient querying and analysis, making it highly suitable for traditional data management systems and analytical tools. See Unstructured Data, Semi-Structured Data.
Supervised Learning	A machine learning approach where a model is trained using labeled data, consisting of input samples and corresponding output labels. The goal is to enable the model to learn the mapping between input features and their corresponding target values. During training, the model generalizes from the labeled data and can predict unseen data by inferring patterns and relationships learned from the training examples. See Unstructured Learning.
TCO	Total Cost of Ownership is a financial metric used to assess the comprehensive costs associated with acquiring, operating, and maintaining a product or system over its entire lifecycle. TCO encompasses not only the initial purchase price but also ongoing operational costs, maintenance expenses, and any costs related to downtime or inefficiency. By providing a holistic view of expenditure, TCO helps organizations make informed decisions about investments, comparing both short-term and long-term implications. See ROI.
TFN	Toll-free numbers are telephone numbers that allow callers to reach businesses or organizations without being charged for the call. The cost of the call is instead borne by the receiving party, usually the business that owns the toll-free number. Businesses, including contact centers, often use these numbers to encourage customer engagement and provide a cost-free channel for customer support, inquiries, or sales.

TPS	Transactions Per Second in an AI interaction refers to measuring how many individual transactions or interactions can be processed by an AI system within one second. It quantifies the system's capacity to handle incoming requests, such as user queries, predictions, or data processing tasks. Higher TPS values indicate a greater ability to handle a larger volume of interactions efficiently, enabling real-time or high-speed AI applications.
TPU	Tensor Processing Units are specialized hardware accelerators designed by Google for machine learning workloads. They excel in processing and manipulating large-scale tensor operations, prevalent in deep learning models. TPUs offer high performance and energy efficiency, enabling faster training and inference times for AI tasks, and they are particularly effective in handling computationally intensive tasks such as neural network training and inference.
Training Data	In predictive machines, training data refers to the labeled dataset used to train a machine learning model. It consists of input samples and their corresponding known output or target values. The model uses Training Data to learn patterns, correlations, and statistical relationships between the input features and the target variable, allowing the model to make accurate predictions on new, unseen data.
Transformative Technology	Innovations that significantly alter the existing market landscape and create new opportunities, often by displacing established technologies or industries. They typically introduce novel approaches, products, or services that offer superior performance, efficiency, or cost-effectiveness compared to traditional solutions. Transformative technologies have the potential to reshape industries, drive market shifts, and bring about transformative changes in business models and consumer behavior.

Transformers	A type of deep learning model architecture that revolutionized natural language processing tasks. They utilize self-attention mechanisms to capture relationships between words or tokens in a sequence, allowing for parallel processing and capturing long-range dependencies. By leveraging attention mechanisms, transformers excel in tasks like machine translation, text generation, sentiment analysis, and more, surpassing the previous sequential approaches and achieving state-of-the-art performance in many language-related tasks.
TSAPI	Telephony Services Application Programming Interface is a set of programming protocols that allows for the integration of computer and telephone systems, commonly employed in Computer Telephony Integration (CTI) environments. Developed by Avaya and Novell, TSAPI enables applications to control and monitor telephony events, facilitating functions such as call routing, queuing, and interactive voice response (IVR). By providing a standardized interface for telephony applications, TSAPI enhances interoperability between different systems and enables more streamlined and efficient communication workflows.
TTS	Text-To-Speech is a technology that converts written text into spoken audio. It involves the synthesis of human-like speech from text input using computational algorithms and linguistic models. TTS systems are utilized in various applications, such as voice assistants, accessibility tools, e-learning platforms, and entertainment, to provide natural and intelligible speech output from written content.

Turing Test	Designed by Alan Turing in 1950, the Turing Test is a test of a computer's ability to display intelligence that is indistinguishable from human intelligence. The test theorized that the software's intelligent behavior could be measured against human intellectual efficiency. The software is intelligent when a human does not know if they are chatting with the software or with another human. Unfortunately, access to computers combined with their functional limitations blocked the development of any proof of concept until recently.
Unstructured Data	Information that lacks a predefined schema or structure, making it challenging to categorize, query, or analyze through conventional database algorithms. This type of data often includes text, images, videos, and audio files, among other formats, which do not fit neatly into tabular structures like rows and columns. Due to its complexity and lack of organization, specialized tools and techniques, such as natural language processing or machine learning algorithms, are often required to analyze and extract meaningful insights from unstructured data. See Structured Data, Semi-Structured Data.
Unsupervised Learning	A machine learning approach where the model learns patterns and structures in data without explicitly labeled examples. It aims to uncover hidden relationships, clusters, or patterns within the input data. Unlike supervised learning, there are no predefined target labels, and the model relies on inherent structures or similarities in the data to identify meaningful insights and make sense of the data. See Structured Learning.

VAR	Variational Autoencoders are generative models in artificial intelligence that combine elements of both autoencoders and probabilistic models. They aim to learn a compact and continuous latent representation of input data by simultaneously training an encoder and decoder network. VAEs introduce a probabilistic approach to autoencoders, allowing for the generation of new data samples by sampling from the learned latent space, making them useful for tasks like data generation, dimensionality reduction, and unsupervised learning.
Voice Bot	An artificial intelligence system that interacts with users through voice commands and responses. Also known as a voice assistant or voice-enabled chatbot. It leverages natural language processing and speech recognition technologies to understand and interpret spoken input. Voice bots are commonly used in applications like virtual assistants, customer support, and smart home devices, offering a hands-free and intuitive way to access information and perform tasks using voice interactions.
Voice-First	Where the voice interaction takes precedence over other forms of input, such as text or touch, and is prioritized as the primary mode of communication between the customer and the system.
VR	Virtual Reality is the technology that creates simulated environments and experiences, often using computer-generated visuals and audio. It aims to immerse users in a virtual world, stimulating their senses and enabling interactive experiences. AI techniques can be employed in VR systems to enhance aspects such as realistic graphics, natural language interactions, and intelligent behavior of virtual entities, making the virtual experience more immersive and engaging.

VUI	Voice User Interface is a technology that allows users to interact with a system through voice or speech commands rather than traditional input methods like touch, keyboard, or mouse. VUIs are increasingly employed in customer service applications in contact centers. The primary objective of a VUI is to provide a more natural, efficient, and accessible means for users to engage with technology, often leveraging artificial intelligence and natural language processing to understand and respond to user requests.
Wake Word	Also known as a trigger word or hot-word, the term refers to a specific word or phrase that acts as a signal to activate a voice-controlled system or virtual assistant. It is a starting point for initiating a conversation or interaction with the system. Request technologies listen for user input in a continuous process. This analyzes audio or text data to detect if the wake word has been spoken or mentioned. Once the wake word is recognized, the system activates and begins capturing and processing subsequent commands or queries. Well-known examples of a wake word are "Hey Siri" in Apple products and "Alexa" used by Amazon.
WFM	Workforce Management is the systematic process that involves planning, scheduling, and monitoring the allocation of human resources to ensure optimal efficiency and productivity within an organization. It encompasses a range of activities, including demand forecasting, staff scheduling, time and attendance tracking, and performance evaluation. By integrating these elements, workforce management aims to balance operational requirements with employee capabilities, thereby enhancing organizational performance and employee satisfaction.

XAI	Explainable AI is an approach in artificial intelligence that emphasizes the transparency and interpretability of AI models and their decision-making processes. It aims to provide understandable explanations for the outcomes or predictions generated by AI systems. By enabling humans to comprehend and trust the reasoning behind AI decisions, explainable AI promotes accountability, fairness, and the identification of potential biases or errors in the decision-making process.
XML	Extensible Markup Language is a text-based markup language that enables the structured representation of data. Developed by the World Wide Web Consortium (W3C), XML provides a way to encode documents or data fields, often using tags to delineate and nest information hierarchically. While not specific to any particular software or hardware, XML is highly extensible and serves as a common standard for data interchange between disparate systems, supporting a wide range of applications in fields such as web development, document storage, and data transmission.
XR	Mixed Reality is the merging of real and virtual worlds to create new environments and visualizations where physical and digital objects coexist and interact in real-time. It combines virtual reality (VR) and augmented reality (AR) elements, allowing users to interact with virtual objects while maintaining a connection to the real world. AI technologies play a significant role in MR by enabling object recognition, spatial mapping, and real-time tracking, enhancing the realism and responsiveness of the mixed-reality experience.

References

Introduction

1. What is the Role of Planning in Artificial Intelligence? (2019). *GeeksforGeeks*. https://www.geeksforgeeks.org/what-is-the-role-of-planning-in-artificial-intelligence/

2. AI and machine learning: It may not be as difficult as you think. (2022). *RSM*. https://rsmus.com/insights/services/digital-transformation/ai-and-machine-learning-it-may-not-be-as-difficult-as-you-think.html?cmpid=ppc:dt-data-analytics-enterprise-ai-ml-g:bb01&gad=1&gclid=Cj0KCQjwqs6lBhCxARIsAG8YcDgqiFv9ZXCjyjTbyd4FCd23Jz1Zitw7mBgil-GClzDm-FV17S452TRsaAlTZEALw_wcB

3. Idoine, C. (2018). Citizen Data Scientists and Why They Matter. *https://blogs.gartner.com/carlie-idoine/2018/05/13/citizen-data-scientists-and-why-they-matter/*

4. Why You Should Care About Augmented Analytics. (2021). *Inteliment*. https://www.inteliment.com/insights/why-you-should-care-about-augmented-analytics/

5. Professional Certificate Course on Business Analytics- Turning into Citizen Data Scientists. (2023). *The Hong Kong Management Association*. https://www2.hkma.org.hk/short/ec-40636-2023-2-l/

Rule 1. Start Your Plan

6. AI Project Life Cycle: Important Stages and Details. (2022). *MaxinAI*. https://www.maxinai.

com/blog/2021/04/12/understanding-ai-project-cycle-important-stages-details/#:~:text=Generally%2C%20 the%20AI%20project%20consists,Stage%20III%2D%20 Deployment%20and%20maintenance

Rule 2. Define Your Business Goals

7. Mominur. (2023). Exploring the Advantages of Chat-GPT: The Ultimate AI-powered Language Model. *Tech-TubeBD*. https://techtubebd.com/artificial-intelligence/ exploring-the-advantages-of-chatgpt-the-ultimate-ai-powered-language-model/

8. Solving AI's ROI problem. It's not that easy. (2021). *PwC*. https://www.pwc.com/us/en/tech-effect/ai-analytics/artificial-intelligence-roi.html

9. AI and 6 Impacts on Shopify, E-commerce, and Revolutionizing Shipping Claims. (2023). *Shipaid*. https://www. shipaid.com/blog/ai-and-6-impacts-on-shopify-e-commerce-and-revolutionizing-shipping-claims

10. Gareiss, R. (2020). AI improves customer experience, call center efficiency. *Customer Experience*. https:// www.techtarget.com/searchcustomerexperience/tip/AI-improves-customer-experience-call-center-efficiency

Rule 3. Outline Your AI Technology Goals

11. Kelly, J. (2023). How to Transform to an AI-Based Call Center. *Invoca Blog*. https://www.invoca.com/blog/ transform-ai-based-call-center

12. Hammond, M. (2021). How to Incorporate AI into Your Call Center Technology. *Aceyus*. https://www.aceyus.com/ how-to-incorporate-ai-into-your-call-center-technology/

13. Maximizing Customer Engagement with Contact Center AI. (2023). *BotPenguin*. https://botpenguin.com/blogs/ maximizing-customer-engagement-with-contact-center-ai

Rule 4. Understand AI Terminology

14. The path to artificial general intelligence. (2021). *Accenture.* https://www.accenture.com/us-en/insights/technology/artificial-general-intelligence

15. Benefits of Using Call Center AI Software. (2023). *Feaed.* https://www.feaed.org/1809/benefits-of-using-call-center-ai-software.html

16. How can GANs be used to generate realistic and diverse text and speech for natural language processing?. (2023). *LinkedIn.* https://www.linkedin.com/advice/1/how-can-gans-used-generate-realistic#:~:text=GANs%20offer%20numerous%20advantages%20for,datasets%20or%20create%20new%20content

17. Burke, J. (2023). Assessing different types of generative AI applications. *Enterprise AI.* https://www.techtarget.com/searchenterpriseai/tip/Assessing-different-types-of-generative-AI-applications?Offer=abMeterCharCount_var1

18. Bell, E. (2023). Artificial General Intelligence (AGI): Definition, How It Works, and Examples. *Investopedia.* https://www.investopedia.com/artificial-general-intelligence-7563858#Types%20of%20Artificial%20General%20Intelligence%20(AG%20Research

19. What is Strong AI?. (n.d.). *IBM.* https://www.ibm.com/topics/strong-ai

20. Progress in AGI Development Raises Concerns About Its Impact on Society. (2023). *The Pakistan Affairs.* https://thepakistanaffairs.com/progress-in-agi-development-raises-concerns-about-its-impact-on-society/

Rule 5. Plan What AI Technologies to Use

21. Clark, S. (2023). Generative AI Solutions for the Contact Center. *CMSWire.* https://www.cmswire.com/contact-center/generative-ai-solutions-for-the-contact-center/

22. Giles, M. (2018). The GANfather: The man who's given machines the gift of imagination. *MIT Technology Review.* https://www.technologyreview.com/2018/02/21/145289/the-ganfather-the-man-whos-given-machines-the-gift-of-imagination/

23. Machine Learning (ML) in Business: Automation and More. (n.d.). *Artsyl.* https://www.artsyltech.com/blog/Machine-Learning-in-Business

24. What is a Cloud Contact Center?. Overview, Benefits, Features. (2023). *TemplateBulb.* https://www.templatebulb.com/what-is-a-cloud-contact-center-overview-benefits-features/

Rule 6. The Essence of GAI and GAN

25. Barla, N. (2023). Generative Adversarial Networks and Some of GAN Applications: Everything You Need to Know. *Neptune.ai.* https://neptune.ai/blog/generative-adversarial-networks-gan-applications

26. Burke, J. (2023b). Successful generative AI examples and tools worth noting. *Enterprise AI.* https://www.techtarget.com/searchenterpriseai/tip/Successful-generative-AI-examples-worth-noting

27. Giles, M. (2018b). The GANfather: The man who's given machines the gift of imagination. *MIT Technology Review.* https://www.technologyreview.com/2018/02/21/145289/the-ganfather-the-man-whos-given-machines-the-gift-of-imagination/

Rule 7. Generative AI Will Transform Customer Service

28. Makarenko, E. (2023). How Conversational AI Is Changing The Way Businesses Communicate. *Master of Code Global.* https://masterofcode.com/blog/how-conversational-ai-is-changing-the-way-businesses-communicate

29. Revolutionizing Customer Interaction: The Future of AI Chatbots with ChatGPT4. (2023). *Canon support downloads.* https://www.canonsupportdownloads.com/2023/04/The-Future-of-AI-Chatbots-with-ChatGPT4.html

Rule 8. Select Your AI Domains

30. The Domains in Artificial Intelligence: Unlocking the Wonders of AI. (2023). *IABAC.* https://iabac.org/blog/the-domains-in-artificial-intelligence

31. Maddula, S. (2021). Domains of AI. *Medium.* https://suryamaddula.medium.com/domains-of-artificial-intelligence-8046d0778f1a

Rule 9. Detail Your AI Domain Descriptions

32. Maddula, S. (2021b). Domains of AI. *Medium.* https://suryamaddula. medium.com/domains-of-artificial-intelligence-8046d0778f1a

33. Task 1: Select priority explanations by considering the domain, use case and impact on the individual. (n.d.). *ico.* https://ico.org.uk/ for-organisations/uk-gdpr-guidance-and-resources/artificial-intelligence/explaining-decisions-made-with-artificial-intelligence/part-2-explaining-ai-in-practice/task-1-select/

34. Sundarajan, S. (2023). Understanding AI Domains. *Cimatri.* https:// cimatri.com/understanding-ai-domains/

35. Feng, C. (2022). Best Practices for Creating Domain-Specific AI Models. *KDnuggets.* https://www.kdnuggets.com/2022/07/best-practices-creating-domainspecific-ai-models.html

Rule 10. Outline Your AI Project Lifecycle

36. Saltz, J. (2023). What is the AI Life Cycle?. *Data Science Process Alliance.* https://www.datascience-pm.com/ai-lifecycle/

37. Maddula, S. (2021c). The AI Project Cycle. *Medium.* https://suryamaddula.medium.com/the-ai-project-cycle-e363ce3f4f6f

38. Understanding and managing the AI lifecycle. (n.d.). *IT Modernization Centers of Excellence.* https://coe.gsa.gov/coe/ai-guide-for-government/understanding-managing-ai-lifecycle/

Rule 11. Plan Your Technology Sequence of Actions

39. Digital transformation in contact centers. (n.d.). *FrontLogix.* https:// frontlogix.com/digital-transformation-in-contact-centers/

Rule 12. Plan Your Sequence of Actions for Business

40. Unlock Your Construction Potential. (2023). *BOSS Magazine.* https:// thebossmagazine.com/construction-project-management-software/

Rule 13. Assess Your Contact Center

41. Decision Analyst Launches New Company To Help Firms Analyze Customer Feedback. (2014). *Survey Magazine*. http://market-researchbulletin.com/decision_analyst_launches_new_company_help_firms_analyze_customer_feedback/index.html

Rule 14. Understand Your Business Objectives

42. McGlynn, C. (2023). How Artificial Intelligence is Changing the Contact Center. *Fonolo*. https://fonolo.com/blog/2023/01/artificial-intelligence-changing-contact-center/

43. Karatella, S. (2023). How AI is Revolutionizing the Call Center Industry. *Call Center Guys*. https://www.callcenterguys.com/blog/how-ai-is-revolutionizing-the-call-center-industry

Rule 15. Understand Your Costs

44. Contact Center Operation and Management. (2023). *Digital.gov*. https://digital.gov/resources/contact-center-guidelines/contact-center-operation-and-management/

Rule 16. Separate ACD and IVR Functionality

45. McGlynn, C. (2023b). How Artificial Intelligence is Changing the Contact Center. *Fonolo*. https://fonolo.com/blog/2023/01/artificial-intelligence-changing-contact-center/

Rule 17. Consider AI for Call Routing

46. A Comprehensive History of AI in the Call Center. (2018). *CallMiner*. https://callminer.com/blog/comprehensive-history-ai-call-center-acds-predictive-analytics-beyond#:~:text=The%20first%20ACD%20systems%20are,this%20technology%20in%20the%20U.K.

47. The Design Switch That Revolutionized Telephone Communications. (2013). *Slate Magazine*. https://www.slate.com/blogs/the_eye/2013/10/03/strowger_switch_the_19th_century_design_invention_that_flipped_the_phone.html

Rule 18. Define Your AI-Powered Performance Indicators

48. McGlynn, C. (2023c). How Artificial Intelligence is Changing the Contact Center. *Fonolo.* https://fonolo.com/blog/2023/01/artificial-intelligence-changing-contact-center/

49. Davis, L. (2022). 11 Essential Call Center Metrics And KPIs (2024 Guide). *Forbes Advisor.* https://www.forbes.com/advisor/business/software/call-center-metrics/

50. Measuring Chatbot Effectiveness. (n.d.). *Visiativ.* https://www.visiativ.com/en/actualites/news/measuring-chatbot-effectiveness/

51. Ashenden, P. (2021). 12 Contact Center KPIs and Metrics for Customer satisfaction. *Lifesize.* https://www.lifesize.com/blog/key-contact-center-kpis/

52. What is KPI (Key Performance Indicator)?. (n.d.). *NICE.* https://www.nice.com/glossary/what-is-contact-center-kpi-key-performance-indicator

53. Felder, I. *The Definitive List of 29 Call Center Metrics and KPIs.* (2022). *Genesys.* https://www.genesys.com/blog/post/the-definitive-list-of-29-call-center-metrics-and-kpis

Rule 19. Prepare for Data Collection

54. Jyoti, R. (2022). Scaling AI/ML Initiatives: The Critical Role of Data. *IDC.* https://www.snowflake.com/wp-content/uploads/2022/03/Scaling-AI-ML-The-Critical-Role-of-Data.pdf

55. Data Collection. (n.d.). *DataRobot.* https://www.datarobot.com/wiki/data-collection/

56. Mahmood, R., Lucas, J., Alvarez, J., Fidler, S., & Law, M. (2022). Optimizing Data Collection for Machine Learning. *Nvidia.* https://research.nvidia.com/labs/toronto-ai/LearnOptimizeCollect/

Rule 20. Identify Your Data Sources

57. Javaid, S. (2023). 5-Step AI Data Collection Process & Roadmap in 2023. *AIMultiple.* https://research.aimultiple.com/data-collection-process/

58. Data Collection + Evaluation. (n.d.). *People + AI Guidebook*. https://pair.withgoogle.com/chapter/data-collection/

59. Noonan, H. (2023). Machine Learning 101: Why and How to Manage Your Customer Data for ML. *Tealium*. https://tealium.com/blog/artificial-intelligence/machine-learning-101-why-and-how-to-manage-your-customer-data-for-ml/

Rule 21. Redact Your Data

60. Federated Learning: The Shift from Centralized to Distributed On-Device Model Training. (2022). *AltexSoft*. https://www.altexsoft.com/blog/federated-learning/

61. Raza, M. (2023). Federated Learning in AI: How It Works, Benefits and Challenges. *Splunk*. https://www.splunk.com/en_us/blog/learn/federated-ai.html

Rule 22. Categorize Your Data Types

62. Structured vs. Unstructured Data: What's the Difference?. (2021). *IBM*. https://www.ibm.com/blog/structured-vs-unstructured-data/

63. Alam, I. (2023). Structured, Semi Structured and Unstructured Data. *K21Academy*. https://k21academy.com/microsoft-azure/dp-900/structured-data-vs-unstructured-data-vs-semi-structured-data/

64. Classification. (n.d.). *Encord*. https://encord.com/glossary/classification-definition/

Rule 23. Federated Learning

65. Martineau, K. (2022). What is federated learning?. *IBM*. https://research.ibm.com/blog/what-is-federated-learning

66. Baracaldo, N., & Ludwig, H. (2022). *Federated Learning: A Comprehensive Overview of Methods and Applications* (1st ed.). Springer Cham. https://link.springer.com/book/10.1007/978-3-030-96896-0?sap-outbound-id=16BFC9D016E1362FE8EBF8CE2B237EB41D020D14#about-this-book

Rule 24. Do You Need Deep Learning?

67. Needle, F. (2021). Deep Learning vs. Machine Learning and How Brands Use Both in Customer Service. *HubSpot.* https://blog.hubspot.com/service/ai-customer-service

68. Deep Machine Learning in AI - Volume: 1. (n.d.). *Education.* https://vocal.media/education/deep-machine-learning-in-ai-volume-1

69. Deep Learning vs. Machine Learning: A Beginner's Guide. (2023). *Coursera.* https://www.coursera.org/articles/ai-vs-deep-learning-vs-machine-learning-beginners-guide

Rule 25. Integrating a Large Language Model

70. Kerner, S. M. (n.d.). Definition: large language models (LLMs). *WhatIs.* https://www.techtarget.com/whatis/definition/large-language-model-LLM

71. Lee, A. (2023). What Are Large Language Models Used For? *NVIDIA.* https://blogs.nvidia.com/blog/2023/01/26/what-are-large-language-models-used-for/

72. What is a Large Language Model (LLM)?. (n.d.). *Elastic.* https://www.elastic.co/what-is/large-language-models

Rule 26. Choose a Voice Persona

73. Mielke, C. (2016). Conversational Interfaces: Where Are We Today? Where Are We Heading?. *Smashing Magazine.* https://www.smashingmagazine.com/2016/07/conversational-interfaces-where-are-we-today-where-are-we-heading/

74. Voice User Interface: Shaping the Future of Interaction. (2023). *Medium.* https://medium.com/theymakedesign/voice-user-interface-a2254208cb4f

75. How Digital Agencies Can Help You Build a Strong Brand Identity. (n.d.). *Dextel Agency* . https://www.dextel.agency/how-digital-agencies-can-help-you-build-a-strong-brand-identity/

Rule 27. Evaluate AI Vendor Technologies

76. How to Assess Vendor Capabilities While Selecting AI/ML Solutions. (n.d.). *IT Convergence*. https://www.itconvergence.com/blog/how-to-assess-vendor-capabilities-while-selecting-ai-ml-solutions/#:~:text=The%20vendor's%20expertise%20and%20experience,in%20your%20industry%20or%20domain

77. Zeal, A. (2023). Tips On How To Choose the Right AI Vendor for Your Business. *Medium*. https://mynameiszeal0.medium.com/tips-on-how-to-choose-the-right-ai-vendor-for-your-business-6b0645898191

Rule 28. Set Expectations for a Proof of Concept

78. Black, C. (2021). 4 Factors for a Successful Proof of Concept. *Medium*. https://medium.com/brainpool-ai/4-factors-for-a-successful-poc-45f856932549

79. How to Implement a Winning AI Proof-of-Concept. (2020). *Novacene AI*. https://novacene.ai/implementing-an-ai-proof-of-concept/

80. Chazareix, A. (2019). How To Build A Successful AI PoC. *Medium*. https://medium.com/sicara/how-to-build-successful-ai-poc-8acfe386a69a

Rule 29. Develop the Criteria for a Proof of Concept

81. Alkhaldi, N. (2023). How creating an AI proof of concept can help you minimize AI development and adoption risks. *ITRex*. https://itrexgroup.com/blog/how-ai-proof-of-concept-helps-you-succeed-in-your-ai-endeavor/#:~:text=An%20artificial%20intelligence%20proof%20of,and%20likely%20to%20be%20successful

82. Storyteller, W. (2022). 9 Essential Keys for a Successful Proof of Concept Evaluation. *Worthwhile*. https://worthwhile.com/insights/2022/11/digital-proof-of-concept-evaluation-criteria/

Rule 30. Plan PoC Use Cases

83. Chazareix, A. (2019b). How To Build A Successful AI PoC. *Medium*. https://medium.com/sicara/how-to-build-successful-ai-poc-8acfe386a69a

84. Alkhaldi, N. (2023b). How creating an AI proof of concept can help you minimize AI development and adoption risks. *ITRex*. https://itrexgroup.com/blog/how-ai-proof-of-concept-helps-you-succeed-in-your-ai-endeavor/

Rule 31. Prepare for Challenges

85. Wen, S. (2019). Moving from Engineering to Orchestrating Conversations. *PolyAI*. https://poly.ai/moving-from-engineering-to-orchestrating-conversations/

86. Kulkarni, A. (2023). The Good, The Bad And The Bot: How Chatbot Experiences Can Make Or Break Your Business. *Forbes*. https://www.forbes.com/sites/forbestechcouncil/2023/04/28/the-good-the-bad-and-the-bot-how-chatbot-experiences-can-make-or-break-your-business/?sh=91f322b4708a

87. Tantsiura, P. (2023). 5 Challenges of Chatbots for Business and How to Overcome Them. *The App Solutions*. https://theappsolutions.com/blog/development/challenges-of-chatbots-for-business/

Rule 32. Structure An Approach for Data Readiness

88. Preparing Your Dataset for Machine Learning: 8 Basic Techniques That Make Your Data Better. (2021). *AltexSoft*. https://www.altexsoft.com/blog/datascience/preparing-your-dataset-for-machine-learning-8-basic-techniques-that-make-your-data-better/

89. Dilmegani, C. (2023). Data Management in '23: What It Is & How Can AI Improve It?. *AIMultiple*. https://research.aimultiple.com/data-management/

Rule 33. Integrate, Engineer, and Format Your Data

90. Preparing Your Dataset for Machine Learning: 8 Basic Techniques That Make Your Data Better. (2021b). *AltexSoft*. https://www.altexsoft.com/blog/datascience/preparing-your-dataset-for-machine-learning-8-basic-techniques-that-make-your-data-better/

91. Dilmegani, C. (2023b). Data Management in '23: What It Is & How Can AI Improve It?. *AIMultiple*. https://research.aimultiple.com/data-management/

Rule 34. Maintain Post-Preparation Data Quality

92. Bhardwaj, S. (2022). Monitoring Machine Learning Models. *Walk-ingTree Technologies*. https://walkingtree.tech/monitoring-machine-learning-models/

Rule 35. Gauge the Success of Your PoC

93. Alkhaldi, N. (2023c). How creating an AI proof of concept can help you minimize AI development and adoption risks. *ITRex*. https://itrexgroup.com/blog/how-ai-proof-of-concept-helps-you-succeed-in-your-ai-endeavor/

94. Black, C. (2021b). 4 Factors for a Successful Proof of Concept. *Medium*. https://medium.com/brainpool-ai/4-factors-for-a-successful-poc-45f856932549

Rule 36. Refine Your PoC for Process Improvement

95. Brownlee, J. (2023). A Gentle Introduction to k-fold Cross-Validation. *MachineLearningMastery*. https://machinelearningmastery.com/k-fold-cross-validation/

96. What is Hyperparameter Tuning?. (n.d.). *Amazon Web Services, Inc.* https://aws.amazon.com/what-is/hyperparameter-tuning/#:~:text=computationally%20intensive%20process.-,What%20are%20hyperparameters%3F,set%20before%20training%20a%20model

97. Kundu, R. (2022). F1 Score in Machine Learning: Intro & Calculation. *V7*. https://www.v7labs.com/blog/f1-score-guide

98. Ajudiya, J. (2021). Data Science ☐☐ | Visual Programming with Orange Tool. *Medium*. https://18it003.medium.com/data-science-visual-programming-with-orange-tool-7ec2ba9eac6f

Rule 37. Plan a Human-AI Mechanism

99. Lasry, B., & Kobayashi, H. (Eds.). (2018). Human Decisions: Thoughts on AI. *Netexplo Notebooks*. https://unesdoc.unesco.org/ark:/48223/pf0000261563

100. What are effective AI solutions for customer escalation management?. (2023). *LinkedIn*. https://www.linkedin.com/advice/0/what-effective-ai-solutions-customer-escalation

Rule 38. Plan for Security

101. Hu, Y., Kuang, W., Qin, Z., Li, K., Zhang, J., Gao, Y., Li, W., & Li, K. (2021). Artificial Intelligence Security: Threats and Countermeasures. *ACM Computing Surveys*, 55(1), 1–36. https://doi.org/10.1145/3487890

102. Marr, B. (2023). The 15 Biggest Risks Of Artificial Intelligence. *Forbes*. https://www.forbes.com/sites/bernardmarr/2023/06/02/the-15-biggest-risks-of-artificial-intelligence/?sh=5fb5000b2706

Rule 39. Address Conversational AI Ethics

103. Security and Ethics of Contact Center AI: When is AI Creepy?. (2021). *NICE*. https://www.nice.com/blog/security-and-ethics-of-contact-center-ai-when-is-ai-creepy

104. Ethics of Chatbots. (n.d.). *Codecademy*. https://www.codecademy.com/article/ethics-of-chatbots

105. Clark, S. (2021). Conversational AI: Creating a Framework of Ethics and Trust. *CMSWire*. https://www.cmswire.com/digital-experience/conversational-ai-creating-a-framework-of-ethics-and-trust/

106. Southern, M. G. (2023). Is Google Collecting Children's Data For Ads? New Report Sparks Concern. *Search Engine Journal*. https://www.searchenginejournal.com/is-google-collecting-childrens-data-for-ads-new-report-sparks-concern/494218/#close

107. Latson, J. (2015). The Woman Who Made History by Answering the Phone. *Time*. https://time.com/4011936/emma-nutt/

Rule 40. Scale Your Solution

108. Collin-Demers, J. (2019). How to Scale your Proof of Concept. *LinkedIn*. https://www.linkedin.com/pulse/how-scale-your-proof-concept-jo%C3%ABl-collin-demers/

109. Kanioura, A., & Lucini, F. (2020). A Radical Solution to Scale AI Technology. *Harvard Business Review.* https://hbr.org/2020/04/a-radical-solution-to-scale-ai-technology

Rule 41. Plan Ongoing Governance and Oversight

110. How can you ensure AI governance and oversight?. (2023). *LinkedIn.* https://www.linkedin.com/advice/1/how-can-you-ensure-ai-governance-oversight

111. Silverman, K. (2020). Why Your Board Needs a Plan for AI Oversight. *MIT Sloan Management Review.* https://sloanreview.mit.edu/article/why-your-board-needs-a-plan-for-ai-oversight/

Rule 42. Continually Innovate

112. Contact Center AI. (n.d.). *DialPad.* https://www.dialpad.com/features/contact-center-ai/

113. Anderson, J., & Rainie, L. (2018). Artificial Intelligence and the Future of Humans. *Pew Research Center.* https://www.pewresearch.org/internet/2018/12/10/artificial-intelligence-and-the-future-of-humans/

114. Lederer, T. (n.d.). Revolutionizing Customer Service: The Role of AI-Powered Contact Center Solutions. *Unify.* https://unify.com/en/blog/revolutionizing-customer-service-the-role-of-ai-powered-contact-center-solutions

115. Extrapolation in Machine Learning (n.d.). *Javatpoint.* https://www.javatpoint.com/extrapolation-in-machine-learning

Appendix A. Assess Your ACD

116. What Is a Cloud Contact Center: Benefits & How It Works. (2023). *Cebod Telecom.* https://www.cebodtelecom.com/what-is-a-cloud-contact-center-benefits-how-it-works/

117. What is ACD (Automatic Call Distribution)?. (n.d.). *RingCentral.* https://www.ringcentral.com/contact-center/automatic-call-distribution.html

118. Bhattacharya, G. (2023). Transform Your Customer Service Approach with AI Assistance: The Key to Success. *Involve.ai.* https://www.involve.ai/post/transform-your-customer-service-approach-with-ai-assistance-the-key-to-success

119. Transform your customer service with our AI-driven contact center software. (n.d.). *Aloware.* https://aloware.com/bot/

Appendix B. Assess Your IVR

120. Robinson, J. (2022). Introduction to Call Centre Processes. *Call Centre Helper.* https://www.callcentrehelper.com/introduction-to-call-centre-processes-52555.htm

About the Author

Geoffrey A. Best started in the computer industry in the 1970s and has worked with contact centers for over 30 years. His career has taken him from computer-aided mapping and 911 emergency dispatch systems to computer telephony applications and today's contact center systems. Geoffrey has worked and consulted worldwide with utilities, communications, manufacturing, banking, and insurance companies. His experience has given him insight into companies' systems and methods to operate their contact centers and service their customers effectively. This experience has given Geoffrey a unique perspective on how customer expectations have changed over the past decades and how contact center solutions have evolved to satisfy them. His latest book introduces how the use of artificial intelligence will impact contact center operations and this new technology's impact on the customer experience.